ACHIEVEMENT
ENGLISH @YEAR 13
CLOSE READING OF
UNFAMILIAR TEXT

NELSON
A Cengage Company

Australia • Brazil • Mexico • Singapore • United Kingdom • United States

Achievement English @ Year 13: Close reading of Unfamiliar Text
1st Edition
Jenny Thomas
Diane White

Typeset: Book Design Ltd
Production controller: Siew Han Ong
Reprint: Alice Kane

Any URLs contained in this publication were checked for currency during the production process. Note, however, that the publisher cannot vouch for the ongoing currency of URLs.

Acknowledgements
Our grateful thanks to all past and present colleagues who have so generously shared their expertise, creativity and resources. English departments thrive on your collegiality.

The authors and publisher wish to thank the following people and organisations for permission to use the resources in this textbook. Every effort has been made to trace and acknowledge all copyright owners of material used in this book. In most cases this was successful and copyright is acknowledged as requested. However, if any infringement has occurred the publishers tender their apologies and invite the copyright holders to contact them. Page 8, Auckland University Press for Under the Pines by Rhian Gallagher; page 16, Longacre Press for *Fire and Ice* by Tania Roxborogh; page 23, Colin Rowbotham for *Dissection*; page 31, Penguin Books (UK) and *The Power and the Glory* by Graham Greene; page 32, ALIVE and Southern Cross for *Our Evolving Language* by Max Cryer; page 35, David Hill for *Zero Tolerance on Holiday roads? What a good idea*; page 38, Frank Sargeson Trust and Random House for *Memoirs of a Peon* by Frank Sargeson; page 40, The Estate of Eric Blair for *Down and Out in Paris and London* by George Orwell; page 42, Auckland University Press for *Along Rideout Road That Summer* by Maurice Duggan; page 48, Penguin Books (UK) for *Cider with Rosie* by Laurie Lee; page 55, Enitharmon Press for *A Case of Murder* by Vernon Scannell; page 58, Faber and Faber (UK) for *An Arundel Tomb* by Philip Larkin; page 62, Faber and Faber (UK) for *Metaphors* by Sylvia Plath; page 66, Farrar, Straus and Giroux for *Death of a Naturalist* by Seamus Heaney; page 68, Elizabeth Smither for *My parents dancing*; page 70, Random House for *You're Telling Me* by Emma Neale.

For product information and technology assistance,
in Australia call **1300 790 853**;
in New Zealand call **0800 449 725**

For permission to use material from this text or product, please email
aust.permissions@cengage.com

National Library of New Zealand Cataloguing-in-Publication Data
A catalogue record for this book is available from the National Library of New Zealand.

Cengage Learning Australia
Level 7, 80 Dorcas Street
South Melbourne, Victoria Australia 3205

Cengage Learning New Zealand
Unit 4B Rosedale Office Park
331 Rosedale Road, Albany, North Shore 0632, NZ

For learning solutions, visit **cengage.co.nz**

Printed in China by China Translation & Printing Services.
2 3 4 5 6 7 8 22 21 20 19 18

Contents

1 Year 13.
Congratulations, you have made a great decision!

By choosing to continue your study of English language and literature into NCEA Level 3, you will complete your secondary education with some really useful communication skills.

You have spent several years in your English classroom learning to recognise language techniques and to understand and appreciate how writers use these techniques to achieve specific purposes.

Achievement English @ Year 13 is designed as a workbook for you to use personally to support your study of English in Year 13. It will assist in the development of your ability to:

- read text with understanding
- analyse text with insight
- express ideas about text with clarity.

Achievement English @ Year 13 is not a book about assessment. It is designed to help you develop all round as a student of English. However, the exercises we have chosen keep NCEA internal and external Achievement Standards in mind.

We are confident that you are ready to begin, so let's get going . . .

ISBN 9780170373319

Year 13 is different

English counts

Next year you will be moving into tertiary education or training, or starting your first full-time job. The most desirable general skills for all students and employees are communication skills.

The ability to listen carefully, to write well and to speak effectively is important.

The ability to analyse and research is also very important.

If you can ...

- **understand** the issues,
- **gather** useful information,
- **sort out** what is valuable and what is irrelevant
- and **offer** sound opinions based on appropriate information,

... then you will be more successful, whatever path you take in your life.

Studying English will help you to achieve these skills and assist your next step, whether it's into a job or tertiary education.

Add your own **jottings, notes, ideas** from class discussions as you work through this book in school or at home.

This book is yours.
WRITE ON IT!

ISBN 9780170373319

Congratulations! 5

2. Close Reading – learning to analyse significant aspects of unfamiliar text

Don't Panic!

This Achievement Standard worries some students because it seems a bit of a mystery. Remember you are preparing for it whenever you read a novel, a short story or a poem and look at the way it has been crafted. You can practise the way to approach an unfamiliar text and this is what we are setting out to do in this part of *Achievement English @ Year 13*.

This book *prepares* you for assessment. It's going to teach you, to remind you about the skills you need to be successful in this assessment. We haven't just chosen easy literature, you might be challenged by some of the material from classic texts. There's plenty of time to read a text over and over, to annotate, to think and to write a response in a 60 minute assessment.

Most of us need a method to approach this Standard successfully. If you approach an unfamiliar text without a method and without having practised that method, you are unlikely to pass. But if you have a method, and you have practised using it regularly then you will pass with flying colours! We know this to be true …

We also know that lots of students begin by thinking 'I can't do this one' but if that's you, then you are wrong!

It's not scary, it's not difficult. What it is, is Achievable – with Merit or Excellence!

ISBN 9780170373319

Check it!

Let's just assure ourselves that you have the basics.

Things to do with prose ...

This extract is taken from *The Voyage*, a short story by Katherine Mansfield. Read it carefully, at least twice, and think about what the writer is intending to achieve with her writing. When you have read the passage, find at least one example of each listed feature or term.

Adjectives	Ellipsis	Oxymoron	Simile
Adverb	Listing	Personification	Effective syntax
Alliteration	Onomatopoeia	Repetition	Verbs

The Picton boat was due to leave at half-past eleven. It was a beautiful night, mild, starry, only when they got out of the cab and started to walk down the Old Wharf that jutted out into the harbour, a faint wind blowing off the water ruffled under Fenella's hat, and she put up her hand to keep it on. It was dark on the Old Wharf, very dark; the wool sheds, the cattle trucks, the cranes standing up so high, the little squat railway engine, all seemed carved out of solid darkness. Here and there on a rounded wood-pile, that was like the stalk of a huge black mushroom, there hung a lantern, but it seemed afraid to unfurl its timid, quivering light in all that blackness; it burned softly, as if for itself.

Fenella's father pushed on with quick, nervous strides. Beside him her grandma bustled along in her crackling black ulster; they went so fast that she had now and again to give an undignified little skip to keep up with them. As well as her luggage strapped into a neat sausage, Fenella carried clasped to her her grandma's umbrella, and the handle, which was a swan's head, kept giving her shoulder a sharp little peck as if it too wanted her to hurry ... Men, their caps pulled down, their collars turned up, swung by; a few women all muffled scurried along; and one tiny boy, only his little black arms and legs showing out of a white woolly shawl, was jerked along angrily between his father and mother; he looked like a baby fly that had fallen into the cream.

ISBN 9780170373319

Things to do with poetry ...

This is a poem by Rhian Gallagher. Read the poem carefully and then complete the task that follows.

Find, highlight and annotate as many examples of the following as you can:

Alliteration	Repetition
Simile	Cliché
Metaphor	Senses
Onomatopoeia	

Under the Pines

Their fine green packed in to make a dark
and this drew me on
round the lagoon. Paddocks open, swept with sunlight
and the pines
serious as a church.

I still hear their boughs
creaking like steps on stairs in depths of night.
Closer in the needles clarified
and the sound became a mast that might not hold.

To walk off the edge of the green world
and into their dust bowl,
that crypt-like half-shadowed temperature,
and once again
to stand there.

Resin scent rinsed like a sharp shower, tingled long after.
Not moving an inch,
myself to myself become a mystery.

Rhian Gallagher

ISBN 9780170373319

Close Reading – let's recap the basics

As a student in Year 13 English you bring with you a wealth of knowledge that you have acquired over several years of study. You read, you listen, you watch with understanding. You have learnt to recognise and appreciate good writing. At this level you are learning to use your knowledge, develop it a little further and apply it to more sophisticated text in an assessment situation.

You will be expected to:

- Respond critically to at least one of each of the following text types:
  - Prose, e.g. persuasive, journalistic, literary
  - Poetry.
- Respond critically to both ideas and language features in unfamiliar texts.
- Communicate ideas and comments clearly and coherently.
- Answer questions that will require short and/or extended written responses.

Close reading prose and poetry

When you 'close read' a piece of writing, whether it is prose or poetry, you are using not only the understanding you have about the content of the piece but also your knowledge of the way writing works. In an assessment of your close reading skills you will be asked to demonstrate your ability to respond to what is written by applying both your knowledge and your response to the text in the answers that you write.

Approaching a passage for close reading

1   Organise your time to give all the questions your calm attention – avoid last minute rushed responses.

2   Always read the whole passage or poem at least twice before you begin so that you can look for the message or purpose of the whole passage.

REMEMBER TO:
1 Read
2 Think
3 Plan
4 Organise
5 Illustrate

3   Ask yourself what type of text it is – oral? written? fiction? non-fiction?

4   Think about each answer before you begin to write.
Short purposeful responses are much better than long, rambling ones – and they save time in an assessment situation.
Don't confuse short and purposeful with short and generalised.

5   Take note of the title. There are often clues to meaning, mood and angle in the title of the poem or extract.

6   There are also clues in the questions. Read each question very carefully.
Unpack it. Highlight (or underline) the key words of instruction and content.
Has it got two parts? If so, be sure to answer both clearly. For example:
   Identify and quote an example of TWO different poetic devices used in the first stanza. Explain the effect created by these.
The answer to this question should have **six** parts: a short quotation (perhaps underlining the words signifying the specific device), a label for the device used in the quotation, and an explanation of the effect of the use of the device – times two.

ISBN 9780170373319

7 Follow the instructions in each question.

- If the question tells you to write **'in your own words'** DO NOT quote from the text.
- If it says **'use specific evidence'** quote the relevant part of the text – not several lines or sentences, hoping that the marker will believe you do know which are the relevant words.
- If it demands that you identify and quote then you must do BOTH.
- If the question asks for one example and you give several, the marker will consider only the first one.
- If the question asks for differences and similarities look for BOTH and organise your answer.

8 Know the terminology. English is no different from other subjects. There is a short-hand of words to describe things. You should KNOW that:

- point of view refers to first, second, third person narration
- syntax means sentence structure
- tense refers to verbs not mood
- infinitive is not the same as imperative and so on ...

Remember, the Language Lists on pages 155-163 are designed to remind you of things that you do know but may have forgotten ...

9 Explain your answer clearly and to the point. **'Explain the effect'** needs a response that is specific to the passage. Try to avoid weak, generalised responses such as 'it makes it sound interesting' or 'it sticks in your mind'.

10 Illustrate your points with examples.

11 Finally, THE most important thing to do is ANSWER THE QUESTION. If you are aiming for Excellence you will need to make sure that your answers not only discuss features of language used but also consider how they contribute to the overall tone, impact, purpose etc of the passage.

ISBN 9780170373319

⊦–◉ First and foremost

The whole of this book has one simple,

fundamental premise ...

... that you will read the text

more than once!

Let's remind you why:

Simple/initial reading

The first time you read a text, whether it is a passage or a poem, an article or a column, a novel, short story or play, you read for meaning and understanding. You follow the ideas or the argument, the description or basic progression of the text. You begin to comprehend its content, you understand the piece as a whole entity and you react, perhaps with curiosity, or interest or intrigue or amusement and you allow yourself to explore, to think about its subject.

Close/analytical reading

When you read the text again, you read to look for and think about its style and effectiveness. Being aware of your understanding of the content and reactions to it, you begin to assess HOW the passage has presented these ideas and prompted these reactions. You interpret, evaluate and discuss the methods the passage uses to convey its meaning.

ISBN 9780170373319

The essentials

The essential elements of successful close reading are:

- understanding the question fully
  and
- understanding the text fully.

You will remember that these are the basic questions that you should be able to answer about any text that you are evaluating, whether it be familiar, unfamiliar, prose, poetry, oral or visual.

1 What is it about?

Essentially this question is asking for an explanation of the subject or topic of a piece.

But what is it *really* about?

In the study of English the word 'theme' or idea is often used, too. Your answer should look more deeply at the text. For example, a short story might be 'about' an old man robbed on his way home, but on a deeper level its theme might be the collapse of a society's values.

2 What is its purpose?

This question wants to know what (you think) the author's intention is. Purpose can be divided simply into categories like:

- To persuade
- To entertain
- To promote an action or thought
- To inform
- To amuse.

But often there is more than one purpose behind a text. Writers sometimes want to change the way we see things, want to make familiar things seem new.

3 What is its tone?

You will have the clues to the tone of the text through things like the writer's choice of words and sentence structure (syntax).

But, you may be asked about the writer or director's style. The choice of vocabulary, sentence structure and figurative language creates the style of a text and parts of a text. It may be a passage from a sci-fi novel with much jargon and action or a poem about a child's world, full of imagery and descriptive detail.

4 Who is the intended audience?

Where written text is concerned 'audience' means readers.

This question wants to know what kind of person you think the piece has been written for.

But, some things can appeal to different audiences on different levels. A novel like *The Lion, the Witch and the Wardrobe* can be read by a child for its adventure story and by an adult for its religious imagery/references.

ISBN 9780170373319

Effective annotation

Annotation is a key skill to being efficient in your analysis of text, whether it be as part of your study of a piece of literature or an extract for close reading. In fact, annotation is something that you will use in all your studies, whether at school, university or training for a job. It helps you as you work to completely understand what you read.

We would expect you to do the following:

Read a passage/poem quietly to yourself (or listen to the teacher read it aloud).

Read it again and:

○ Check you understand the vocabulary. Do you know what all the words mean?

○ Highlight words you don't understand and use a dictionary to give you clear, appropriate meanings

○ Write these definitions on the page

Read it again (yes, a third time!) annotating key features:

○ Figurative language like similes and metaphors

○ Effective words or phrases

○ Special sentence structures

ISBN 9780170373319

- ○ Details that may answer specific questions

- ○ Links between different parts of the text

- ○ Anything you see as interesting/ important

- ○ Think about the tone created in the passage. How is it created?

- ○ Is there a particular style? How is it created?

- ○ What do these things add to your understanding?

What to do with the annotations

After this 'technical read', look at how these things you have noted work for the passage as a whole. Are they building an image or a character? Is a setting being created? Are they revealing to you a specific mood or atmosphere? Are they persuading you? Making you laugh?

These detailed, annotated notes will create the basis of any discussion or written work you are asked to do on a text.

Putting all this into practice

Use all of these suggestions to help you fully understand and appreciate the following text. It is an extract from *Third Degree*, a novel by Tania Roxborogh. Read it carefully, at least twice, and think about what the writer is intending to achieve with her writing.

Fire and Ice

When they ask me, I say I cannot remember. But, in my dreams, I am breathless with laughter running down the hall with someone chasing me. I will be caught soon. I am running into the lounge, I grab a hold of the kitchen door, the panelled door; cream, with scrubbed out paint on the edge. My fingers lock into the lip of one panel and I glance quickly back down the lit hall. The others are coming. I laugh, and using the door, and my fingers, I swing, I sweep around toward the kitchen.

I see grey and feel my cheek and top lip crush into grey. Hard, metal grey. I see stars and then the burning starts and my eyes are squeezed tight so the pain cannot get into them but the heat scratches my face, my hair. Rough hands pull me and I hear cries and calls and voices from under water and I am standing in the middle of the living room now.

A child is screaming and screaming somewhere but, when I look, the other children are silent. I hear the screaming but I can only make sounds in my head because it hurts so much. Mum is speaking to me but I don't hear her words. I only sense her fear and see her bravery as she takes my pants off, my socks off, my shirt off.

But, I call to her in my head, but Mum, the boys will see me naked. They will see me. Mum doesn't hear because she is mouthing sounds as she carries me to the bathroom and into the bath.

On the outside, the water is ice-cold but on the inside, it burns and burns and I want to get out. I try to get out but big rough, big sore hands are holding me down. Hot and cold. Heat and ice. Burning and freezing.

"Please let me out", the sound comes out of my mouth. "I would like to get out now", I say politely knowing that manners will always get me places. So, I am out. Shivering from the heat and the cold. Shivering. Shaking. Silently shivering and shaking as I am taken back to the kitchen.

ISBN 9780170373319

I spy a grey metal pot and spilt water; its fire has already seeped away into the floor, leaving only a wet trail. Mum opens the oven door while Dad talks on the phone. "Come closer", she says.

"I can't", I croak, my lips wrestling with me; my cheeks stubbornly refusing to move. "I'm hot". But I am still shaking so they ignore me and pull me closer to the heat. The wave of oven-heat reaches out its scratchy hand and strokes me, rips me and I bleed clear drops onto the bare floor.

Tania Roxborogh

First ...

Annotate the extract looking for examples of:

- Alliteration
- Metaphor
- Passive verb
- Repetition
- Contrasting words
- Minor sentence
- Personal pronoun
- Simile
- Effective verbs
- Oxymoron
- Personification.

Now answer these straightforward questions in as much detail as possible. Use quotations and references to the text to support your ideas.

1 What do you know about the narrator from this passage? Support your answer with evidence from the text.

_____

_____

_____

_____

_____

_____

2 What techniques has the author used to create the sense of panic and pain in the passage?

_____

_____

_____

_____

_____

_____

ISBN 9780170373319

Digging deeper

This is a famous poem, possibly one of the most extensively studied in the English language. It was written by William Blake in 1794 before we knew much about exotic wild animals. Does spelling the word 'tiger' as *tyger* make it seem even more ancient and mysterious? You will easily find Blake's original, illustrated version of this poem on the Internet.

The Tyger

Tyger Tyger burning bright,
In the forests of the night;
What immortal hand or eye
Could frame thy fearful symmetry?

In what distant deeps or skies
Burnt the fire of thine eyes?
On what wings dare he aspire?
What the hand, dare seize the fire?

And what shoulder, & what art,
Could twist the sinews of thy heart?
And when thy heart began to beat
What dread hand? & what dread feet?

What the hammer? what the chain,
In what furnace was thy brain?
What the anvil? what dread grasp
Dare its deadly terrors clasp?

When the stars threw down their spears
And watered heaven with their tears:
Did he smile his work to see?
Did he who made the Lamb make thee?

Tyger Tyger burning bright,
In the forests of the night:
What immortal hand or eye,
Dare frame thy fearful symmetry?

William Blake

ISBN 9780170373319

First …

Annotate the poem looking for examples of:

- Alliteration
- Effective imagery
- Metaphor/Personification
- Repetition
- Rhetorical questions
- Rhyme
- Rhythm
- Significant pronouns
- Symbolism.

This poem rhymes. Count the syllables in each line and work out the rhyme pattern. Your teacher may show you how this poem is written in a (mostly) trochaic rhythm. We do not look at analysing rhythm (scansion) in depth because most students will not meet it in class. However, you can look it up on the Internet. We even found a website where you can identify rhythm patterns online http://prosody.lib.virginia.edu/.

When you think you understand the meaning of the poem, answer the following questions in as much detail as possible. Use quotations and references to the text to support your ideas.

1 In the first verse why does the tiger burn bright?

_____

_____

2 How many questions does the poet ask? Are they linked?

_____

_____

3 In verse 4 what image does the poet use for the creator of the tiger? Why?

_____

_____

_____

_____

4 What does he finally want to know? Think about what the words 'he' and 'Lamb' represent in religious imagery. (Look it up if you don't know.)

_____

_____

_____

_____

_____

_____

_____

_____

_____

Scaffolding an answer

The end result of much of your close reading at this level is to have ideas to offer in a class discussion or answer questions – usually in writing.

Involving yourself in class discussion is an excellent way to improve your understanding of a text. We do appreciate, though, that writing answers to questions is usually where your results come from, so let's think about the question for a moment.

The most important thing is make sure that you understand what the question is asking you to write. After all, there isn't much point filling up the allocated lines but not actually giving the information the examiner requires.

Achievement English @ Year 13 continues to help develop your strategies for close reading unfamiliar text.

You have written answers to what are commonly called 'scaffolded questions'. You will recollect that a scaffold is a support structure, usually around a building being developed. However, when talking about a scaffolded question in English it refers to a question that offers you support, or hints, as to how to answer the question. Such a question will demand a longer, more detailed and self-structured answer.

This takes more effort, especially in planning your answer.

You understand that scaffolded questions will not ask about an isolated technique or meaning or purpose. Instead, they will ask a wider question but will give you ideas about how to answer them in depth and detail. Always use the clues to complete your answer as fully as possible.

So what does this mean?

- Instead of being given several short, specific questions you are given one or two more general questions.
- These questions demand a longer, more structured answer.
- At Year 13 you will usually be expected to plan the structure of your response yourself. There may be clues/key words in the question itself to guide you.

Is that important?

- Your answer will be assessed as N, A, M or E depending on the detail in the response you provide.
- Show that you have heeded what you have learned about longer answers in previous years by planning your answer carefully.
- Your aim is a response that clearly expresses your understanding of the text.

ISBN 9780170373319

Here is an example of the kind of question we are talking about:

Explain how the writer develops a sense of chaos. Refer to specific techniques from the text to support your answer.

This question directs you to a specific idea in the text but requires you to select for yourself appropriate language techniques (more than one is required) to comment on.

How do you tackle this kind of question?
Like any other question you are asked!

You are very familiar with answering very specific short questions relating to text. *Why is the word 'xxx' used? What does this metaphor suggest?* etc. You have also had considerable experience of longer, more holistic questions by now.

As with any other question, the key thing is that you actually answer the question. Writing an answer of sufficient length is probably not an issue, but getting enough depth and detail might be something you need to work on.

Use this strategy to help you

- ○ Read the question twice.
- ○ Underline key words.
- ○ Read and re-read the passage.
- ○ Underline or highlight detail that looks important to you as you go.
- ○ Make annotations to help you find appropriate parts of the passage or techniques you have noticed easily.
- ○ Take the time to plan your answer. Think of it as a small essay.
- ○ Make sure you are using specific language terminology.
- ○ Check that you always support any point you make with an example.
- ○ Write your answer.
- ○ Re-read your answer – have you answered the question?

Practising your skills

In this next section we are going to look at two methods of approaching a text.

> **METHOD 1**
>
> A series of questions focussed on different aspects of the poem.

> **METHOD 2**
>
> A general question where you scaffold the structure of a longer answer yourself.

Both these methods require you to have closely read and understood the whole poem or passage.

Before you go any further let's look at the poem we will base this comprehension on, *Dissection* by Colin Rowbotham.

A poet often writes from his or her own experiences. This poem was written by a student about your age to examine an experience in a school science class. You may find that you can appreciate his experience, especially if you have been in a similar position.

The poem is easy to understand. Read it aloud and it will sound like someone speaking his thoughts aloud. Think about the way the poet shows you what he is doing and then invites you to follow his thoughts to wonder at what he discovers, and then to his conclusion about the point of his learning.

Remember, before you answer any questions you should have read the poem at least three times and made relevant annotations.

First ...

- Where does the poet appeal to some of your senses?
- Identify the similes and metaphors the poet has used and their effect.
- Suggest reasons why some of the lines are short and why some words are placed out of usual grammatical sequence.
- Think about why punctuation marks are used.
- Look for onomatopoeia, assonance, imperative, alliteration, analogy.

Using what you have now observed about the poem you should be able to write detailed answers to the questions.

ISBN 9780170373319

Dissection

This rat looks like it is made of marzipan,
Soft and neatly packaged in its envelope;
I shake it free,
Fingering the damp, yellow fur, I know
That this first touch is by far the worst.

    There is a book about it that contains
Everything on a rat, with diagrams
Meticulous, but free from blood
Or all the yellow juices
I will have to pour away.

    Now peg it out:
My pins are twisted and the board is hard
But, using force and fracturing its legs,
I manage though
And crucify my rat.

    From the crutch to the throat the fur is ripped
Not neatly, not as shown in the diagrams,
But raggedly;
My hacking has revealed the body wall
As a sack that is fat with innards to be torn
By the inquisitive eye
And the hand that strips aside.

    Inside this taut elastic sack is a surprise;
Not the chaos I had thought to find,
No oozing mash; instead of that
A firmly coiled discipline
Of overlapping liver, folded gut;
A neatness that is like a small machine –
And I wonder what it is that has left this rat,
Why a month of probing could not make it go again,
What it is that has disappeared ...

    The bell has gone; it is time to go for lunch.
I fold the rat, replace it in its bag,
Wash from my hands the sweet
Smell of meat and formalin
And go and eat a meat pie afterwards.

    So, for four weeks or so, I am told,
I shall continue to dissect this rat;
Like a child
Pulling apart a clock he cannot mend.

Colin Rowbotham

Method 1:

1 What is the poet inviting the reader to do in this poem?

_____

_____

_____

_____

_____

_____

_____

2 How does the poet appeal to the reader's senses?

_____

_____

_____

_____

_____

_____

_____

3 Explain to what effect several literary techniques are used in the poem.

_____

_____

_____

_____

_____

_____

_____

_____

ISBN 9780170373319

4   Examine the theme of the poem as revealed in the final three lines.

_____

_____

_____

_____

_____

_____

_____

_____

5   What is your opinion of this theme?

_____

_____

_____

_____

_____

_____

_____

_____

_____

Method 2:

Discuss the language techniques used in the poem. Why are they important features of the work?

If you are given a single question requiring a longer answer to respond to you might use a grid like this as a planning device (a scaffold) after you have read the poem, thought about it and completed your annotations. A plan can lead to a more carefully constructed response.

Plan:

Idea 1	personal pronouns, imperative
Idea 2	simile and metaphor
Idea 3	alliteration, onomatopoeia, assonance
Idea 4	emotive words – especially verbs and adverbs

Sample grid for Idea 1:

Topic	Example	Description/ deconstruction	Explanation	Evaluation
Personal pronouns	'I shake it free' 'I know that this first touch …' 'I manage though and crucify' 'I had thought'	Describes the narrator's actions. Leads reader through the events and introduces narrator's thoughts.	Structures the poem chronologically and focuses on the personal actions and response of the narrator.	Works well. Understand he is not proficient, dislikes the task but is nevertheless completing it and being provoked into thought by it.
Imperatives	'I am told' 'Now peg it out'	Suggests a situation of compulsion.	Tells reader the setting of the poem – a classroom.	

Sample paragraph based on these ideas:

In *Dissection* Colin Rowbotham uses the first person pronoun 'I' to lead the reader through the action of the poem. 'I shake it free', 'I know/That this first touch is by far the worst'. We can follow the dissection of the rat and the poet's poor skills as he describes his imperfect actions and his feelings. 'I manage and crucify my rat', 'not the chaos I had thought to find'.

'Now peg it out' is an instruction, clearly putting the actions into a classroom setting. He is following a teacher's directions, doing what he is told to do, not what he wants to do. These techniques work well because the reader understands that the narrator is not proficient and that he dislikes this task that he is obliged to complete.

ISBN 9780170373319

Have a go:

Choose one of the other ideas listed in the plan on page 26 and complete the grid below.

Topic	Example	Description/ deconstruction	Explanation	Evaluation

Now write your own paragraph/s based on these ideas:

_____

_____

_____

_____

_____

_____

_____

_____

_____

_____

_____

_____

_____

_____

_____

_____

_____

_____

5 Text type 1: Prose

You should know by now that a 'prose' text is anything that is written that is not poetry. You will be expected to examine an infinite variety of prose text – from a novel to a blog to a ... The techniques writers use are the same, to achieve that variety of outcomes. You know that you have to read a text more than once, you know lots of terminology to express your analysis well.

Terminology you should be confident with ...

You are in your final year of studying prose at school and by now you know it is important to include the technical language of English in your answer. The list below is what we would expect you to know at this level.

You will notice in the left hand margin there are two circles labelled 'I know' and 'I need to check'. Read through the list and tick the box that best describes your knowledge of each literary term. Look up all the ones you don't know in the Language Lists at the end of this book.

I know	I need to check		I know	I need to check		I know	I need to check	
○	○	Abstract noun	○	○	Denotation	○	○	Personification
○	○	Adjective	○	○	Emotive language	○	○	Preposition
○	○	Adverb	○	○	Euphemism	○	○	Pronoun
○	○	Alliteration	○	○	Extended metaphor	○	○	Pun
○	○	Allusion	○	○	Hyperbole	○	○	Repetition
○	○	Assonance	○	○	Imagery	○	○	Rhetorical question
○	○	Cliché	○	○	Irony	○	○	Sentence construction
○	○	Collective noun	○	○	Jargon	○	○	Simile
○	○	Colloquial language	○	○	Metaphor	○	○	Slang
○	○	Common noun	○	○	Narrative voice	○	○	Superlative
○	○	Comparative adjective	○	○	Noun	○	○	Syntax
○	○	Conjunction	○	○	Onomatopoeia	○	○	Tense
○	○	Connotation	○	○	Parts of speech	○	○	Verb

ISBN 9780170373319

We thought we would remind you about:

Denotation/connotation

Denotation is the dictionary meaning of a word. Connotation is the implied or suggested meaning. For example, the word 'mother' denotes one who has given birth. However the word 'mother' may have the connotation of female, caring, sensible, loving, practicality, experience, homemaker and so on.

Why? Because writers choose their vocabulary extremely carefully and they often expect their reader to understand the connotations of the words they choose. They expect their reader to work with them and to bring a certain level of understanding of the connotations of the words they use.

Extended metaphor

An extended metaphor takes an idea and develops it through a passage or poem.

Why? Because there will be some in the literature you study this year – without question!

Emotive language

Emotive language is the deliberate use of words to exaggerate, describing a subject or an event to interest the reader or listener in a way that will excite the emotions.

Emotive words are used extensively in persuasive writing and speaking to convince others of an author's point of view, often on a controversial issue. They express bias, a tendency towards a particular point of view or preference.

Why? Because writers are trying to get a response from their readers and the ones who do this most successfully will be the ones who are chosen for you to study this year.

Syntax

Syntax is the arrangement, organisation and relationship of words, phrases and clauses in sentences.

Why? Because writers, especially those writing fiction, tend to use syntax for purposes other than conveying information and sometimes break the 'rules' quite deliberately for effect.

For revision of syntax see pages 142-154.

The language of prose

To sum up, this chart draws together all of the terminology you will use as you close read prose. Use it as a reference whenever you look at a piece of unfamiliar prose text.

HOW DO WE APPROACH A PIECE OF UNFAMILIAR PROSE?

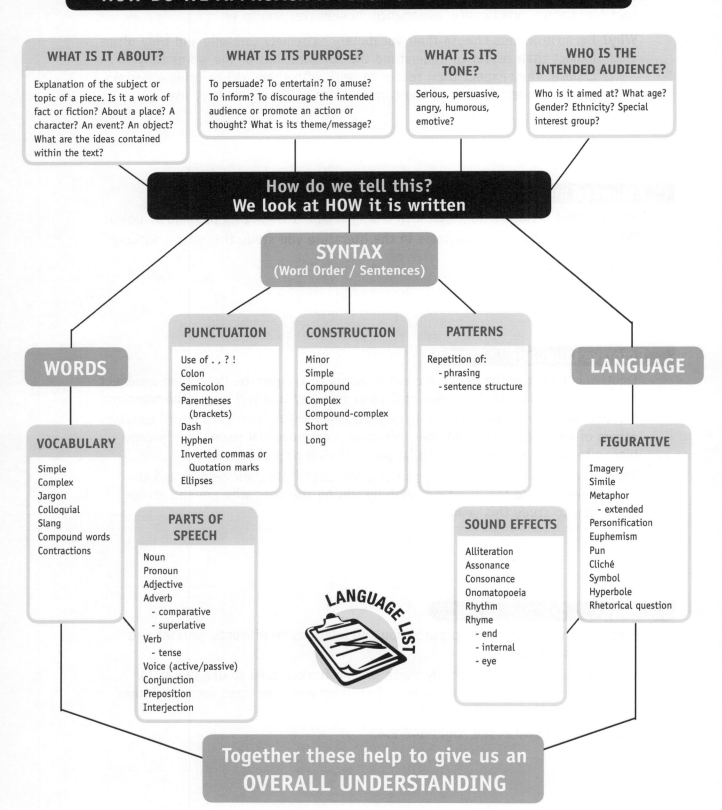

WHAT IS IT ABOUT?

Explanation of the subject or topic of a piece. Is it a work of fact or fiction? About a place? A character? An event? An object? What are the ideas contained within the text?

WHAT IS ITS PURPOSE?

To persuade? To entertain? To amuse? To inform? To discourage the intended audience or promote an action or thought? What is its theme/message?

WHAT IS ITS TONE?

Serious, persuasive, angry, humorous, emotive?

WHO IS THE INTENDED AUDIENCE?

Who is it aimed at? What age? Gender? Ethnicity? Special interest group?

How do we tell this?
We look at HOW it is written

SYNTAX
(Word Order / Sentences)

PUNCTUATION

Use of . , ? !
Colon
Semicolon
Parentheses
   (brackets)
Dash
Hyphen
Inverted commas or
   Quotation marks
Ellipses

CONSTRUCTION

Minor
Simple
Compound
Complex
Compound-complex
Short
Long

PATTERNS

Repetition of:
- phrasing
- sentence structure

WORDS

LANGUAGE

VOCABULARY

Simple
Complex
Jargon
Colloquial
Slang
Compound words
Contractions

PARTS OF SPEECH

Noun
Pronoun
Adjective
Adverb
   - comparative
   - superlative
Verb
   - tense
Voice (active/passive)
Conjunction
Preposition
Interjection

LANGUAGE LIST

SOUND EFFECTS

Alliteration
Assonance
Consonance
Onomatopoeia
Rhythm
Rhyme
   - end
   - internal
   - eye

FIGURATIVE

Imagery
Simile
Metaphor
   - extended
Personification
Euphemism
Pun
Cliché
Symbol
Hyperbole
Rhetorical question

Together these help to give us an
OVERALL UNDERSTANDING

ISBN 9780170373319

Let's look at a writer's use of techniques

This is the opening of the famous novel *The Power and the Glory* by Graham Greene.

Start by looking at the way the passage has been constructed. Highlight any use of effective **adjectives, adverbs, verbs.** Look for **onomatopoeia, alliteration** and **repetition.** Notice how the writer uses **punctuation.**

However, a writer does not set out to incorporate as many 'techniques' as possible in his or her prose. He or she wants you to 'see' what is being described. Here the writer uses third person narration to show the reader a man and a location.

Mr Tench went out to look for his ether cylinder: out into the blazing Mexican sun and the bleaching dust. A few buzzards looked down from the roof with shabby indifference: he wasn't carrion yet. A faint feeling of rebellion stirred in Mr Tench's heart, and he wrenched up a piece of the road with splintering finger-nails and tossed it feebly up at them. One of them rose and flapped across the town: over the tiny plaza, over the bust of an ex-president, ex-general, ex-human being, over the two stalls which sold mineral water, towards the river and the sea. It wouldn't find anything there: the sharks looked after the carrion on that side. Mr Tench went on across the plaza.

He said 'Buenos dias' to a man with a gun who sat in a small patch of shade against a wall. But it wasn't like England: the man said nothing at all, just stared malevolently up at Mr Tench as if he had never had any dealings with the foreigner, as if Mr Tench were not responsible for his two gold bicuspid teeth. Mr Tench went sweating by, past the Treasury which had once been a church towards the quay.

Answer the following question in as much detail as possible. Use quotations and references to the text to support your ideas.

What can you tell about this character and the place he is in from these opening lines?

_____

_____

_____

_____

_____

_____

_____

_____

_____

_____

Prose close reading practice

A variety of prose text and accompanying questions are provided in this section to help you practise answering close reading questions.

Text 1

This passage is an extract from a magazine article called *Our Evolving Language* by Max Cryer. Read the following passage. Look up words you don't know the meaning of and annotate important features (see pages 155-163).

Two strange geographic confusions were introduced by local media into New Zealand English: all Oriental people became referred to as Asians – carelessly disregarding that Asia is not a race but a place which includes eastern Russia, India, Afghanistan, Nepal, Bhutan, Tibet, Philippines … none of them Oriental. And Māori people, although they are Polynesian, became excluded from Polynesia – as in 'Māori and Polynesian', which is rather like saying 'New Zealanders and Cantabrians'.

Employers paying employees often changed to contractors paying contractees, but who were referred to as 'contractors' – making some confusion about who was paying whom.

More Māori words have moved into the vernacular and everyday reportage. In 2001 an Australian journalist visiting New Zealand wrote with surprise that he needed a dictionary to read the daily newspaper because so many Māori words were in everyday use.

But enlargement of vocabulary hasn't necessarily meant that New Zealand

English has become more polished in its usage. Many believe teaching the basics of the English language have been sidelined – school exams can now even accept text spelling as correct, as long as the meaning is clear. To many, this seems we can now feel the heat of the approaching handbasket, as hell gets closer.

Perhaps these are some of the reasons why there are constant cries about the New Zealand standard lack of expression. Captains of industry have difficulty spelling, politicians stumble and mispronounce. Signwriters and journalists use that, which and who as if they all meant the same thing and have abandoned any distinction between less and fewer.

A New Zealand cabinet minister came back from a high-level conference in Europe and commented that his equivalents over there moved easily through two or even three languages 'while we were struggling with just one'. Leaders of professions, television presenters and even the prime minster

ISBN 9780170373319

are convinced that the plural of woman is woman.

A busy office can operate without any phone books. An encyclopaedia is no longer a must-have in many households – nor a dictionary. Just use the computer. The University of Auckland (40,000 students) now requires that all entrants without exception sit a test called Diagnostic English Language Needs Assessment. The Post Office has dramatically reduced its letter collections – there are now so few to collect. It could be said we are losing a connection to print – and consequently to literacy.

Even if so, New Zealand English manages to continue doing a language's job – it communicates.

Whatever its future, the daily exchange of New Zealand English retains some rugged individuality. Words from other languages are absorbed without stress: Diwali, feng shui, pizza, perestroika, sushi. Sports players in their late thirties with a university degree and four children are (rather strangely!) called 'boys' and 'girls'. What we call 'whitebait' bears no relationship to the English fish it is named after. Our 'flax' is a mistaken name given to a plant which has no connection with the real flax from which linen is made. Our 'public schools' are what they say they are – for the public.

And we keep things up to the mark with words of our very own. Where would we be without 'perkbusters' and 'whistleblowers'?

Answer the following questions in as much detail as possible. Use quotations and references to the text to support your ideas.

1 The writer contends that NZ English (NZE) is geographically incorrect. In what ways?

_____

_____

2 How has Māori enlarged NZE vocabulary in recent years?

_____

_____

3 What does the underlined sentence mean?

_____

_____

4 What is the cliché being manipulated in paragraph 4? Why is it used?

_____

_____

_____

_____

5 Highlight the examples used to show evidence of poor use of NZE. Is there a link?

_____

_____

_____

6 What, does the writer claim, has replaced the dictionary?

_____

7 What does 'rugged individuality' mean in terms of NZE?

_____

_____

8 Give examples of this 'rugged individuality'.

_____

_____

_____

_____

_____

9 Why is 'rather strangely' in brackets and with an exclamation mark?

_____

_____

_____

10 Overall do you think this writer is in favour of the changes he says are happening to NZE?

_____

_____

_____

_____

_____

ISBN 9780170373319

Text 2

Read the following passage. Look up words you don't know the meaning of and annotate important features (see pages 155-163).

Zero tolerance on holiday roads?
What a good idea

DAVID HILL

Drive carefully, says the protagonist at the end of Aldous Huxley's The Genius and the Goddess. "This is a Christian country and it's the Saviour's birthday. Practically everybody you see will be drunk."

Last month, Transport Minister Paul Swain indicated he wanted to censor the great Kiwi Christmas Story of celebration – inebriation – regurgitation. He proposed *a raft (called a raft because rafts drift directionlessly)* of tough, pre-Christmas road safety measures, including a cut to the legal blood-alcohol level, and targeting of drink-drive teenagers.

The usual *howls of* protest rose. The usual *melee of metaphors* formed. *"A second kick in the teeth,"* claimed a *spokesthing* for the Hospitality Association who also claimed that this Government needs to *pull its head in*. It's true such a cranial retraction would reduce one's chances of being *kicked in the molars,* but that's another story.

Rural objections were heard as well. I don't know much about country life: to me, the country is that bit I dash across to get from the front door to the car door. But I couldn't help being impressed by the farmers' assertions that any threat to their getting *legless in the local* was also a threat to all that is *sacred in our society.*

Like them, I wasn't impressed by Paul Swain's proposals, however. For different reasons, though – I felt they didn't go far enough.

For example, why should we be showing zero tolerance only towards teenagers who drink and drive. *We should have zero tolerance of all teenage activities, including their metabolic processes.* But that's another story, too.

I concede that summer holidays are not an easy time for drivers, who suddenly find themselves on highways *wherecarsarejammedtogetherlikethis.*

But since *'tis the season to curb folly,* and since there are no liberals behind steering wheels, I suggest we extend Mr Swain's intolerance to a degree that would send the Minister of Transport *into transports.*

I'd like to show zero tolerance *to the drivers* of bloke-built holiday homes, especially those which should be preceded by flashing lights and OVERSIZE signs. I want these decent law-abiding folks victimised for two reasons.

First, having worked hard all their lives and now enjoying their totally deserved retirement, they're in absolutely no hurry to get anywhere and can't see why any other driver should be. Second, when they congregate in their holiday-homes-away-from-home *parks, these owners of ROMAN FREE, WAI WORRI and BUG_IT_F_I_NO inevitably start lamenting the decline of literacy and spelling in today's schools.*

I want zero tolerance shown towards *certain cyclists.* These include the racy ones who know they're 10 gears above dreary laws, and who clog the highways with scores *of bobbing black bums.*

Then there are the slow, serene Cape Reinga-to-Bluff cyclists, who pull little trolleys behind their bikes and who ride with a smile on their faces, a song on their lips, a melanoma on their ears. These freedom-wheelers exude such fitness, brightness and smugness that I ache to drive straight over their little trolleys.

I would support minimal tolerance, too, for *Auckland drivers* holidaying in the provinces, who return home and declaim incredulously how they went on this road and it was shingle, and then

they had to swerve because there were these cowpats.

Plus the same severity for *provincial* drivers on holiday in Auckland, who suddenly cross three lanes of the Harbour Bridge because Karlie hasn't seen the Waitemata before.

Let's add *courier van* drivers delivering all those parcels that just made or just missed the Christmas feeding frenzy. Specifically, the courier drivers who treat red lights, yellow lines, *black looks* and *white knuckles* as whimsical irrelevancies.

And we'll include the *family cars* with Jarrod, aged 9, sticking his tongue out in the rear window. Jarrod makes my fingers twitch towards my *bonnet mounted Kalashnikov.*

Why stop at half measures? I want zero tolerance of the *senior station-wagon* so low on its rear springs it seems to be preparing for *sub-orbital flight.*

Continued overleaf …

You can recognise these offenders by the roof-rack overflowing with holiday gear to the point where following drivers are liable to receive Karlie's Bob-the-Builder beach-towel across their front windscreen.

A variant on such vehicles is the *surfie* wagon, from which fibreglass boards with *fins like flensing spades* protrude a metre from windows. A truckie friend has his own zero tolerance policy towards these: he drives close enough to threaten fin amputations. Needless to say, I can't approve...enough.

Although *we never the Swain shall meet*, let's extend his intolerance to cover vehicles whose occupants *toss takeaway food* or drink containers out of the window; vehicles whose drivers still wear *back-to-front baseball caps;* vehicles *towing trailers* of poorly packed garden rubbish whose *cascading contents* turn SH1 into a bush walk.

In a final flurry of kick-in-the-teeth enthusiasm we'll include cars *with personalised plates* reading ALL MYN, BAD BOI or LUSTI, plus cars towing 10 tons of Beach Belle on a bouncing, swinging, road-obscuring trailer to another harbour where they can *moor it opposite the waterfront pub.*

Oh, and cars full of *lawn bowlers* wearing lawn bowlers' hats, who know it's all right to turn out of side streets in front of oncoming traffic because it's only 50m till they turn off again to their motel.

Around here, I start to sense some Automobilis Anonymous muttering that if I had my way, there'd be nobody allowed on our roads. Well, of course. We all know that the only really safe and competent driver around is us. *While others succumb to road rage, we remain a Road Sage.*

But that's another story. ◼

Answer the following questions in as much detail as possible. Use quotations and references to the text to support your ideas.

1 The opening paragraph uses a quotation. It juxtaposes two seemingly incongruous ideas. Explain what these are. How does this quotation lead into the article?

_____

_____

_____

2 Identify two personal pronouns used in this article. Explain why each is used. Quote from the text to support your ideas.

_____

_____

_____

3 This article is written for a New Zealand audience. Apart from the use of certain proper nouns, how can you tell?

_____

_____

_____

4 Which groups did not want the suggested new restrictions? What is the writer's attitude towards those who oppose the new road safety measures? How can you tell?

_____

_____

_____

_____

ISBN 9780170373319

5 Comment on the use of cliche, alliteration, hyperbole and allusion in this article.

i _____

_____

ii _____

_____

iii _____

_____

_____

iv _____

_____

_____

6 Give two examples of the writer using the visual presentation of words to suggest meaning. Explain the meaning of each example.

_____

_____

_____

7 Comment on the use of parentheses in paragraph 2.

_____

_____

_____

8 Comment on the use of demonstratives in paragraph 13, beginning: 'I would support ...'

_____

_____

_____

9 Comment on the use of colours in paragraph 14, beginning: 'Let's add courier ...'

_____

_____

_____

10 In what way does the article differ from what you might expect from its title?

_____

_____

_____

_____

Read the following extract from *Memoirs of a Peon* by Frank Sargeson. It describes a scene in detail involving a poor young man who has become acquainted with the wealthy Gower-Johnson family of Remuera. Look up words you don't know the meaning of and annotate important features (see pages 155-163).

I had not been introduced to Mr Gower-Johnson, but I wondered if I had seen him when I climbed to the lily pool terrace to fetch Mrs Gower-Johnson her favourite parasol which she had left in her favourite clematis-draped summerhouse. A stoutish man, dressed as though for bowls with a waistcoat on underneath his blazer, was standing looking very intently at the pool; and as I passed him I murmured a polite good afternoon without eliciting any sign of a response. But a moment or so later, without removing his eyes from the pool, he called to a workman some distance off – a young man wearing a football jersey who was engaged in weeding one of the many herbaceous borders. I now had the parasol and was again near the pool; and looking too, I saw a frog seated upon one of the lily leaves. It was a somewhat unreal sight: the creature was green, a somewhat lighter shade than the unblemished and perfect leaf it sat upon, but it was so brightly gilded that it might have been a varnished toy in a shop window waiting to be bought for some child. I stopped to watch as the young man approached, and immediately the frog was pointed out to him his hand went to the long sheath-knife he wore on his hip: then he crept swiftly to the rim of the pool from which he suddenly reached out to slash with his knife. The frog disappeared as the water splashed and then bubbled; but just before I turned away the surface was broken by a very tiny frog-hand which looked desperately mute and forlorn as it poked up through the hole where the leaf had been slashed. I ran down the stone steps, and presenting the parasol to Mrs Gower-Johnson I said, "I've just seen a green-and-gold frog sitting on a lily leaf." And she answered, "Oh, have you! They're such a nuisance, they keep us awake at night."

ISBN 9780170373319

Answer the following questions in as much detail as possible. Use quotations and references to the text to support your ideas.

1 Explain what the writer shows you about the Gower-Johnsons and about the young male narrator's relationship with the family.

_____

_____

_____

_____

_____

_____

_____

_____

_____

2 Comment on the language the writer chooses to use to describe this scene. What sort of mood is created?

_____

_____

_____

_____

_____

_____

_____

3 What comment do you think the writer is making about these wealthy urban people through this scene? And might there be a message for the young man in the event he has just witnessed?

_____

_____

_____

_____

_____

Read the following passage from *Down and Out in Paris and London* by George Orwell. Look up words you don't know the meaning of and annotate important features (see pages 155-163).

Our cafeterie was a murky cellar measuring twenty feet by seven by eight high, and so crowded with coffee-urns, breadcutters and the like that one could hardly move without banging against something. It was lighted by one dim electric bulb, and four or five gas-fires that sent out a fierce red breath. There was a thermometer there, and the temperature never fell below 110 degrees Fahrenheit — it neared 130 at some times of the day. At one end were five service lifts, and at the other an ice cupboard where we stored milk and butter. When you went into the ice cupboard you dropped a hundred degrees of temperature at a single step; it used to remind me of the hymn about Greenland's icy mountains and India's coral strand. Two men worked in the cafeterie besides Boris and myself. One was Mario, a huge, excitable Italian — he was like a city policeman with operatic gestures — and the other, a hairy, uncouth animal whom we called the Magyar; I think he was a Transylvanian, or something even more remote. Except the Magyar we were all big men, and at the rush hours we collided incessantly.

The work in the cafeterie was spasmodic. We were never idle, but the real work only came in bursts of two hours at a time — we called each burst 'UN COUP DE FEU'. The first COUP DE FEU came at eight, when the guests upstairs began to wake up and demand breakfast. At eight a sudden banging and yelling would break out all through the basement; bells rang on all sides, blue-aproned men rushed through the passages, our service lifts came down with a simultaneous crash, and the waiters on all five floors began shouting Italian oaths down the shafts. I don't remember all our duties, but they included making tea, coffee and chocolate, fetching meals from the kitchen, wines from the cellar and fruit and so forth from the dining-room, slicing bread, making toast, rolling pats of butter, measuring jam, opening milk-cans, counting lumps of sugar, boiling eggs, cooking porridge, pounding ice, grinding coffee — all this for from a hundred to two hundred customers. The kitchen was thirty yards away, and the dining-room sixty or seventy yards. Everything we sent up in the service lifts had to be covered by a voucher, and the vouchers had to be carefully filed, and there was trouble if even a lump of sugar was lost. Besides this, we had to supply the staff with bread and coffee, and fetch the meals for the waiters upstairs. All in all, it was a complicated job.

I calculated that one had to walk and run about fifteen miles during the day, and yet the strain of the work was more mental than physical. Nothing could be easier, on the face of it, than this stupid scullion work, but it is astonishingly hard when one is in a hurry. One has to leap to and

ISBN 9780170373319

fro between a multitude of jobs — it is like sorting a pack of cards against the clock. You are, for example, making toast, when bang! down comes a service lift with an order for tea, rolls and three different kinds of jam, and simultaneously bang! down comes another demanding scrambled eggs, coffee and grapefruit; you run to the kitchen for the eggs and to the dining-room for the fruit, going like lightning so as to be back before your toast burns, and having to remember about the tea and coffee, besides half a dozen other orders that are still pending; and at the same time some waiter is following you and making trouble about a lost bottle of soda-water, and you are arguing with him. It needs more brains than one might think. Mario said, no doubt truly, that it took a year to make a reliable cafetier.

Answer the following question in as much detail as possible. Use quotations and references to the text to support your ideas.

1 The writer is describing a personal experience in the kitchen of a hotel in Paris. What does he say about the working conditions, the work itself and the qualities required to work there successfully?

NOTE: This is a three part question ... it requires a three part answer!

_____

_____

_____

_____

_____

_____

_____

_____

_____

_____

_____

_____

_____

_____

_____

_____

Read the following passage from *Along Rideout Road That Summer* by Maurice Duggan. Look up words you don't know the meaning of and annotate important features (see pages 155-163).

I'd walked the length of Rideout Road the night before, following the noise of the river in the darkness, tumbling over ruts and stones, my progress, if you'd call it that, challenged by farmers' dogs and observed by the faintly luminous eyes of wandering stock, steers, cows, stud-bulls or milk-white unicorns or, better, a full quartet of apocalyptic horses browsing the marge. In time and darkness I found Puti Hohepa's farmhouse and lugged my fibre suitcase up to the verandah, after nearly breaking my leg in a cattlestop. A journey fruitful of one decision – to flog a torch from somewhere. And of course I didn't. And now my feet hurt; but it was daylight and, from memory, I'd say I was almost   10
happy. Almost. Fortunately I am endowed both by nature and later conditioning with a highly developed sense of the absurd; knowing that you can imagine the pleasure I took in this abrupt translation from shop-counter to tractor seat, from town pavements to back-country farm, with all those miles of river-bottom darkness to mark the transition. In fact, and unfortunately there have to be some facts, even fictional ones, I'd removed myself a mere dozen miles from the parental home. In darkness, as I've said, and with a certain stealth. I didn't consult dad about it, and, needless to say, I didn't tell mum. The moment wasn't propitious; dad was asleep with the Financial Gazette <u>threatening to</u>   20
<u>suffocate him</u> and mum was off somewhere moving, as she so often did, that this meeting make public its whole-hearted support for the introduction of flogging and public castration for all sex offenders and hanging, drawing and quartering, for almost everyone else, and as for delinquents (my boy!) ... Well, put yourself in my shoes, there's no need to go on. Yes, almost happy, though my feet were so tender I winced every time I tripped the clutch.

Almost happy, shouting Kubla Khan, <u>a bookish lad</u>, from the seat of the clattering old Ferguson tractor, doing a steady five miles an hour in a <u>cloud of seagulls</u>, getting to the bit about the damsel with a dulcimer   30
and looking up to see the reputedly wild Hohepa girl perched on the gate, feet hooked in the bars, ribbons fluttering from her ukelele. A perfect moment of recognition, daring rider, in spite of the belch of carbon monoxide from the tin-can exhaust up front on the bonnet. Don't, however, misunderstand me: I'd not have you think we are here embarked on the trashy clamour of boy meeting girl. No, the problem, you are to understand, was one of connexion. How connect the dulcimer with the ukelele, if you follow. For a boy of my bents this problem of how to cope with the shock of the recognition of a certain discrepancy between the real and the written was rather like watching mum with a   40

ISBN 9780170373319

shoehorn <u>wedging nines into sevens</u> and suffering merry hell. I'm not blaming old STC for everything, of course. After all <u>some other imports went wild too</u>; and I've spent too long at the handle of a mattock, a critical function, not to know that. The stench of the exhaust, that's to say, held no redolence of that old hophead's pipe. Let us then be clear, and don't for a moment, gentlemen, imagine that I venture the gross unfairness, the patent absurdity, the rank injustice (your turn) of blaming him for spoiling the pasture or fouling the native air. It's just that there was this problem in my mind, this profound, cultural problem affecting dramatically the very nature of my inheritance, nines into   50 sevens in this lovely smiling land. His was the genius as his was the expression which the <u>vast educational brouhaha</u> invited me to praise and emulate, tranquillizers ingested in maturity, the voice of the ring-dove, look up though your feet be in the clay.

Of course I understood immediately that these were not matters I was destined to debate with Fanny Hohepa. Frankly, I could see that she didn't give a damn; it was part of her attraction. She thought I was singing. She smiled and waved, I waved and smiled, turned, ploughed back through gull white and coffee loam and fell into a train of thought not entirely free of Fanny and her instrument, pausing to wonder, now   60 and then, what might be the symptoms, the early symptoms, of carbon monoxide poisoning. Drowsiness? Check. Dilation of the pupils? Can't check. Extra cutaneous sensation? My feet. Trembling hands? Vibrato. Down and back, down and back, turning again, Dick and his Ferguson, Fanny from her perch seeming to gather about her the background of <u>green paternal acres</u>, fold on fold. I bore down upon her with all the eager erubescence* of youth, with my hair slicked back. She trembled, wavered, fragmented and reformed in the pungent vapour through which I viewed her. (oh for an open-air job, eh mate?) She plucked, very picture in jeans and summer shirt of youth and suspicion, and   70 seemed to sing. I couldn't of course hear a note. Behind me the dog-leg furrows and the bright ploughshares. Certainly she looked at her ease and, even through the gassed up atmosphere between us, too deliciously substantial to be a creature down on a visit from Mount Abora. I was glad I'd combed my hair. Back, down and back. Considering the size of the paddock this could have gone on for a week. I promptly admitted to myself that her present position, disposition or posture, involving as it did some provocative tautness of cloth, suited me right down to the ground. I mean to hell with the idea of having her stand knee-deep in the thistle thwanging her dulcimer and plaintively chirruping about a   80 pipedream mountain. In fact she was natively engaged in expressing the most profound distillations of her local experience, the gleanings of a life lived in rich contact with a richly understood and native environment: A Slow Boat to China, if memory serves. While I, racked and shaken, composed words for the plaque which would one day stand here to commemorate our deep rapport.

*blushing

ISBN 9780170373319

Before answering the questions on the Maurice Duggan passage read the following extracts from the poem *Kubla Khan* by Samuel Taylor Coleridge (1772–1834).

In Xanadu did Kubla Khan

A stately pleasure-dome decree:

Where Alph, the sacred river, ran

Through caverns measureless to man

Down to a sunless sea.

So twice five miles of fertile ground

With walls and towers were girdled round:

And there were gardens bright with sinuous rills,

Where blossomed many an incense-bearing tree;

And here were forests ancient as the hills

Enfolding sunny spots of greenery.

…

…

A damsel with a dulcimer

In a vision once I saw:

It was an Abyssinian maid,

And on her dulcimer she played,

Singing of Mount Abora.

Could I revive within me

Her symphony and song,

To such a deep delight 'twould win me,

That with music loud and long,

I would build that dome in air,

That sunny dome! Those caves of ice!

And all who heard should see them there,

And all should cry, "Beware! Beware!

His flashing eyes, his floating hair!

Weave a circle round him thrice,

And close your eyes with holy dread,

For he on honey-dew hath fed,

And drunk the milk of Paradise."

ISBN 9780170373319

Answer the following questions in as much detail as possible. Use quotations and references to the text to support your ideas.

1   What do you learn about the narrator and his journey from the opening sentence?

_____

_____

2   Comment on the use of the word 'better' in the opening sentence and its link to his comment about a torch.

_____

_____

_____

3   Comment on the syntax of these lines:

'In time and darkness I found Puti Hohepa's farmhouse and lugged my fibre suitcase up to the verandah, after nearly breaking my leg in a cattlestop. A journey fruitful of one decision – to flog a torch from somewhere. And of course I didn't. And now my feet hurt; but it was daylight and, from memory, I'd say I was almost happy. Almost.'

_____

_____

_____

4   What is the effect of the use of personal pronouns?

_____

_____

5   What does he think is absurd?

_____

_____

6   How does the passage appeal to the senses? Give three examples from the text and explain each one's effect.

_____

_____

_____

_____

_____

_____

7 What are his parents like? What is his relationship with them? Support your answer with evidence from the text.

_____

_____

_____

8 Three phrases have been placed in parentheses. Quote each one and explain why it is in parentheses.

_____

_____

_____

_____

_____

9 Explain the meaning of three of these phrases:

threatening to suffocate him *(line 20/21)*   some other imports went wild too *(line 42/43)*
a bookish lad *(line 28)*   vast educational brouhaha *(line 52)*
cloud of seagulls *(line 30)*   green paternal acres *(line 66)*
wedging nines into sevens *(line 41)*

i _____

_____

ii _____

_____

iii _____

_____

10 Give at least two examples of the use of humour in the passage.

i _____

_____

_____

_____

ii _____

_____

_____

_____

ISBN 9780170373319

Now look at how the second text (*Kubla Khan*) relates to the first.

11 Explain in detail what the young man's 'profound cultural problem' is and how it relates to the lines from the poem that he refers to.

What is the writer suggesting about New Zealand's education system in the middle of the 20th century?

_____

_____

_____

_____

_____

_____

_____

_____

_____

_____

_____

_____

_____

_____

_____

_____

_____

_____

_____

_____

_____

_____

Read the following extract from *Cider with Rosie* by Laurie Lee. Look up words you don't know the meaning of and annotate important features (see pages 155-163).

Radiating from that house, with its crumbling walls, its thumps and shadows, its fancied foxes under the floor, I moved along paths that lengthened inch by inch with my mounting strength of days. From stone to stone in the trackless yard I sent forth my acorn shell of senses, moving through unfathomable oceans like a South Sea savage island-hopping across the Pacific. Antennae of eyes and nose and grubbing fingers captured a new tuft of grass, a fern, a slug, the skull of a bird, a grotto of bright snails.

From the harbour mouth of the scullery floor I learned the rocks and reefs and the channels where safety lay. I discovered the physical pyramid of the cottage, its stores and labyrinths, its centres of magic and of the green, sprouting island-garden upon which it stood. My mother and sisters sailed past me like galleons in their busy dresses, and I learned the smells and sounds which followed in their wakes, the surge of breath, carbolic, song and grumble, and smashing of crockery.

The scullery was a mine of all the minerals of living. Here, I discovered water – a very different element from the green crawling scum that stank in the garden tub. You could pump in pure blue gulps out of the ground, you could swing on the pump handle and it came out sparkling like liquid sky. And it broke and ran and shone on the tiled floor or quivered in a jug, or weighted your clothes with cold. You could drink it, draw with it, froth it with soap, swim beetles across it, or fly it on bubbles in the air. You could put your head in it, and open your eyes, and see the sides of the bucket buckle, and hear your caught breath roar, and work your mouth like a fish, and smell the lime from the ground. Substance of magic – which you could wear or tear, confine or scatter, or send down holes, but never burn or break or destroy.

Here too was the scrubbing of floors and boots, of arms and necks, of red and white vegetables. Walk in to the morning disorder of this room and all the garden was laid out dripping on the table. Chopped carrots like copper pennies, radishes and chives, potatoes dipped and stripped clean from their coats of mud, the snapping of tight pea-pods, long shells of green pearls, and the tearing of glutinous beans from their nests of wool.

 ISBN 9780170373319

Answer the following question in as much detail as possible. Use quotations and references to the text to support your ideas.

1   This passage describes a place from a particular point of view. Explain what the words reveal about the narrator himself and about children in general.

Your answer might include some of these points:

- The narrator's world
- How a child's view is different from an adult's
- How the writer uses images that link together
- How the senses provide close observation of things
- How children learn.

_____

_____

_____

_____

_____

_____

_____

_____

_____

_____

_____

_____

_____

_____

_____

_____

_____

_____

_____

_____

_____

_____

_____

_____

An aside on ... style

When the word style is applied to a text it refers to the features of that text that make it typical of an author, a historical period, a particular audience, a genre or kind of text. For instance:

- a humorous style
- a satirical style
- a serious style
- a scientific style

- a didactic style
- a conversational style
- a persuasive style
- a witty style

- a sarcastic style
- an ironic style.

Some possible ways to approach a passage in search of its style

What is the passage about?

- List or highlight the main ideas/topics.

What is the tone of the passage?

- Is it humorous or serious, angry or amusing, satirical or logical? It can be more than one!
- Does it amuse, persuade, inform or entertain you?
- Is it balanced or one-sided? Passionate or dispassionate?
- Is it the writer's own opinion or is there a persona?
- What is the writer's intended effect on the reader?
- What kind of reader is it aimed at?
- What kind of publication is it taken from – a novel? A newspaper? A specialist magazine? A play?

What is the theme of the passage?

- Is there a meaning beyond the basic subject of the passage?
- Are there hidden messages?
- Is there a judgement or a conclusion that the writer leads you to?
- Is it stated explicitly or can you infer meanings?

Once you have some opinions about the subject and theme of the writing, who the audience is, what the writer's attitude is towards that subject, you can go on to look at how the piece achieves its style.

Steps to take

1. What does the **title** tell you?

2. What are the main steps in the **development of the passage's ideas**? Divide the passage into sections.

3. Identify where/how the **sections** are linked, for example, with key words, with similar images, with repeated syntax.

4. Look at the **vocabulary** the writer has chosen. How does it suit the audience, the intention of the piece, the writer's attitude, the tone of the piece. Is the reader involved? How? Look for formal and informal language, for specialised words, for words with connotations, for irony, satire, cynicism, exaggeration for personal pronouns, for neologisms, for slang, for colloquialisms, for allusions to events, or other texts, for personal anecdotes, for figures of speech, for the sound of the words – rhythm, assonance, onomatopoeia, alliteration, etc.

5. Consider **imagery**. Does the piece use imagery (simile, metaphor, personification, litotes, hyperbole, etc)? What for? Symbolism? To suggest or imply meanings or an attitude? To create atmosphere?

6. Look at the **sentence structure**. Short, long or a mixture? Simple or complex? Active or passive? Are there patterns of sentence construction? What conjunctions are used?

Whenever you comment on a passage you are using your knowledge of language devices and your appreciation of how they work to inform your comments on the passage. What you write in response to a question is not naming of parts – to be precise and concise you need the terminology to use to express your ideas with precision.

ISBN 9780170373319

Text type 2: Poetry

If you have been using the *Achievement English* books through your senior schooling, we hope you have grown in confidence in analysing poems and have learnt to enjoy reading poetry.

The beauty of a poem in these classroom and assessment circumstances is that it is a complete piece. There is no guessing what has gone before or what has happened after – the poet has put it all in the one poem.

Poets are deeply interested in words ... in a very few words they evoke emotion, they make us think. Of course it is the specific words they have chosen and the way in which they combine these words that create such powerful effects. That is what you are trying to work out when you analyse poetry. What has the poem made me think and feel? How has it managed to do this?

Because we know that some of you will still be saying 'Urgh' we thought we should repeat the simple advice we have given you previously.

1 **Don't worry.** A poem is not a puzzle that must be deciphered completely before you get the 'right' answer.

A poet spends a lot of time choosing exactly the best words for their poem. You may not understand them all or be able to see why they were chosen. That doesn't mean you cannot understand the idea that the poet is trying to share. Some poems you may be asked to read are written by and for people who have a lot more experience of life than you do at the moment. You can enjoy and understand parts of a poem without fully grasping it all.

2 When you study an unfamiliar text in class you may be given the text on a single sheet for annotation. If not, **make one for yourself** and add your own annotations.

3 Always read a poem lots of times. Try to read it aloud. The first poetry was meant to be spoken, or read aloud, just like children's poems and stories. Make sure you read to the punctuation. Often an idea is not contained in each separate line.

4 Decide what you think the poem is generally about. There may be a simple surface meaning and a deeper one, too. Do this before you begin to look at the way the poet has chosen words and images, has used figures of speech and layout, to deliver that meaning. Sometimes the title can hint at the theme of a poem.

Continued overleaf ...

How to approach a poem

5 Look at the poem in more detail. Always ask yourself why the poet chose those particular words. Often you will be asked questions that guide you towards particular things like figures of speech (simile, metaphor, sound devices), parts of speech (nouns, verbs) and pattern (rhythm, rhyme, sentence structure). At this level it is important that you are able to recognise and name the devices used, but much more important that you can comment on their effect in terms of the poem as a whole. Use a dictionary to look up any words you do not understand.

6 Respond. Think about why you enjoyed the poem. Was it humorous? Did it have something important to say? Was it relevant to your life? Poems mean different things to different people. Your personal response may be different from your classmates, but it is just as valid.

7 Don't worry.
Relax and enjoy as much poetry as you can. Read some for pleasure!

Annotating a poem

A useful way of trying to understand and appreciate a poem is to place a copy of it in the middle of a sheet of paper and annotate your ideas around it.

1 Read the poem aloud if possible, or alternatively listen to someone else read it.

2 Read the poem to yourself several more times as you get confident with its vocabulary, rhythm and flow.

3 Using a quality dictionary, look up the meaning of any words you are unsure of. Annotate these definitions. A dictionary often gives several meanings for a word so you need to pick the meaning that fits the poem.

Look for:

4 the subject

5 the poet's attitude towards the subject, often revealed as 'tone'

6 the theme.

Then look for:

7 images, perhaps created by use of figures of speech

8 effective words (diction, vocabulary)

9 patterns like sentence structure, verses, rhyme.

Then ask yourself:

10 what do I think about the poem and its ideas?

ISBN 9780170373319

Terminology you should be confident with ...

You are in your final year of studying poetry at school and by now it is important to include the technical language of English in your answer. The list below is what we would expect you to know at this level.

You will notice in the left hand margin there are two circles labelled 'I know' and 'I need to check'. Read through the list and tick the box that best describes your knowledge of each literary term. Look up all the ones you don't know in the Language Lists at the end of this book.

I know	I need to check		I know	I need to check		I know	I need to check	
○	○	Alliteration	○	○	Extended metaphor	○	○	Rhyme
○	○	Antithesis	○	○	Imagery	○	○	Rhythm
○	○	Apostrophe	○	○	Metaphor	○	○	Sibilance
○	○	Assonance	○	○	Onomatopoeia	○	○	Simile
○	○	Caesura	○	○	Oxymoron	○	○	Symbolism
○	○	End-stopped line	○	○	Personification			
○	○	Enjambment	○	○	Repetition			

We thought we would remind you about:

Punctuating Poetry

Caesura

A natural pause or a break in a line of poetry, usually indicated by a punctuation mark.
For example: When will the bell ring, and end this weariness?

(D.H. Lawrence, Last Lesson of the Afternoon)

Enjambment

When the meaning of a line of poetry is completed on the next line.
For example: How long have they tugged the leash, and strained apart,
                 My pack of unruly hounds.   *(D.H. Lawrence, Last Lesson of the Afternoon)*
This technique can emphasise an idea or add to the rhythm and flow of the lines.

End-stopped line

The lines of a stanza that have a grammatical pause at the end of each line.
For example: I can haul and urge them no more.   *(D.H. Lawrence, Last Lesson of the Afternoon)*
This technique completes an idea visually and grammatically.

Why? Because if you read the poem to the punctuation then understanding the poem is so much easier.

The language of poetry

To sum up, this chart draws together all of the terminology you will use as you close read poetry. Use it as a reference whenever you look at an unfamiliar poem.

HOW DO WE APPROACH AN UNFAMILIAR POEM?

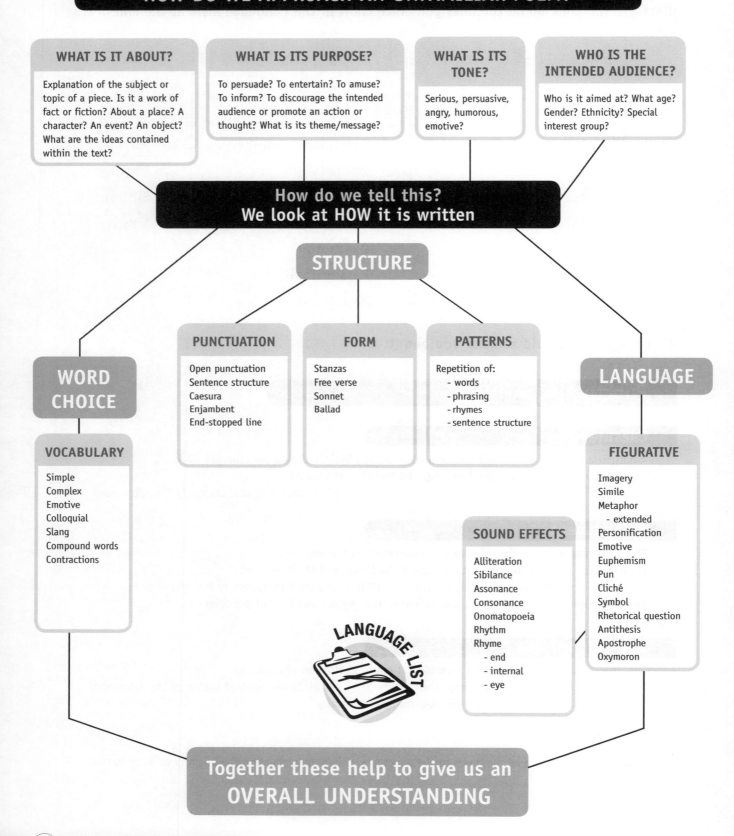

WHAT IS IT ABOUT?

Explanation of the subject or topic of a piece. Is it a work of fact or fiction? About a place? A character? An event? An object? What are the ideas contained within the text?

WHAT IS ITS PURPOSE?

To persuade? To entertain? To amuse? To inform? To discourage the intended audience or promote an action or thought? What is its theme/message?

WHAT IS ITS TONE?

Serious, persuasive, angry, humorous, emotive?

WHO IS THE INTENDED AUDIENCE?

Who is it aimed at? What age? Gender? Ethnicity? Special interest group?

How do we tell this?
We look at HOW it is written

STRUCTURE

PUNCTUATION

Open punctuation
Sentence structure
Caesura
Enjambent
End-stopped line

FORM

Stanzas
Free verse
Sonnet
Ballad

PATTERNS

Repetition of:
- words
- phrasing
- rhymes
- sentence structure

WORD CHOICE

LANGUAGE

VOCABULARY

Simple
Complex
Emotive
Colloquial
Slang
Compound words
Contractions

SOUND EFFECTS

Alliteration
Sibilance
Assonance
Consonance
Onomatopoeia
Rhythm
Rhyme
- end
- internal
- eye

FIGURATIVE

Imagery
Simile
Metaphor
- extended
Personification
Emotive
Euphemism
Pun
Cliché
Symbol
Rhetorical question
Antithesis
Apostrophe
Oxymoron

LANGUAGE LIST

Together these help to give us an
OVERALL UNDERSTANDING

ISBN 9780170373319

Let's look at a poem together

This poem, written by Vernon Scannell, is concerned with a childhood experience. Use the same approach as you did for the prose passages. Poetry and prose use words in much the same ways. However, it is important to read poetry to the punctuation, not to the lines. Read it aloud, if possible – it helps with understanding.

Read the poem carefully several times. As you do so, highlight the end rhymes. Notice the punctuation. Highlight and annotate examples of repetition, simile, metaphor, onomatopoeia and any other language features you notice. See how many words are more than a single syllable.

We have given you some straightforward questions to answer briefly as annotated notes, which will assist you to understand the poem fully. These annotations should help you to form a complete detailed answer to the final question.

A Case of Murder

They should not have left him there alone,
Alone that is except for the cat.
He was only nine, not old enough
To be left alone in a basement flat,
Alone, that is, except for the cat.
A dog would have been a different thing,
A big gruff dog with slashing jaws,
But a cat with round eyes mad as gold,
Plump as a cushion with tucked-in paws---
Better have left him with a fair-sized rat!
But what they did was leave him with a cat.
He hated that cat; he watched it sit,
A buzzing machine of soft black stuff,
He sat and watched and he hated it,
Snug in its fur, hot blood in a muff,
And its mad gold stare and the way it sat
Crooning dark warmth: he loathed all that.

1 Who is 'they'?

_____

_____

2 How old is the child?

_____

3 Description of cat's eyes suggests what?

_____

_____

_____

4 What does he hate about the cat?

_____

_____

_____

_____

So he took Daddy's stick and he hit the cat.

Then quick as a sudden crack in glass

It hissed, black flash, to a hiding place

In the dust and dark beneath the couch,

And he followed the grin on his new-made face,

A wide-eyed, frightened snarl of a grin,

And he took the stick and he thrust it in,

Hard and quick in the furry dark.

The black fur squealed and he felt his skin

Prickle with sparks of dry delight.

Then the cat again came into sight,

Shot for the door that wasn't quite shut,

But the boy, quick too, slammed fast the door:

The cat, half-through, was cracked like a nut

And the soft black thud was dumped on the floor.

Then the boy was suddenly terrified

And he bit his knuckles and cried and cried;

But he had to do something with the dead thing there.

His eyes squeezed beads of salty prayer

But the wound of fear gaped wide and raw;

He dared not touch the thing with his hands

So he fetched a spade and shovelled it

And dumped the load of heavy fur

In the spidery cupboard under the stair

Where it's been for years, and though it died

It's grown in that cupboard and its hot low purr

Grows slowly louder year by year:

There'll not be a corner for the boy to hide

When the cupboard swells and all sides split

And the huge black cat pads out of it.

Vernon Scannell

5　Why is Daddy's stick relevant?

_____

_____

_____

_____

6　Why does the boy grin?

_____

_____

_____

7　What effect do the rhymes, the single syllable words and onomatopeia have on this poem?

_____

_____

_____

_____

_____

_____

_____

_____

_____

8　Why does he cry?

_____

_____

9　Why does the purr grow louder?

_____

_____

10　What does the huge black cat symbolise?

_____

ISBN 9780170373319

Answer the following question in as much detail as possible. Use quotations and references to the text to support your ideas.

What is the poet saying about childhood experiences in this poem?

_____

_____

_____

_____

_____

_____

_____

_____

_____

_____

_____

_____

_____

_____

_____

_____

_____

_____

_____

_____

Remember your annotations will help you scaffold an answer with depth and detail ...

Poetry close reading practice

A variety of poetic text and accompanying questions are provided in this section to help you practise answering close reading questions.

Text 1

Read the following poem. Look up words you don't know the meaning of and annotate important features (see pages 155-163).

An Arundel Tomb

I   Side by side, their faces blurred,
The earl and countess lie in stone,
Their proper habits vaguely shown
As jointed armour, stiffened pleat,
And that faint hint of the absurd—
The little dogs under their feet.

II   Such plainness of the pre-baroque
Hardly involves the eye, until
It meets his left-hand gauntlet, still
Clasped empty in the other; and
One sees, with a sharp tender shock,
His hand withdrawn, holding her hand.

III They would not think to lie so long.
Such faithfulness in effigy
Was just a detail friends would see:
A sculptor's sweet commissioned grace
Thrown off in helping to prolong
The Latin names around the base.

IV They would not guess how early in
Their supine stationary voyage
The air would change to soundless damage,
Turn the old tenantry away;
How soon succeeding eyes begin
To look, not read. Rigidly they

V   Persisted, linked through lengths and breadths
Of time. Snow fell, undated. Light
Each summer thronged the glass. A bright
Litter of birdcalls strewed the same

ISBN 9780170373319

> Bone-riddled ground. And up the paths
> The endless altered people came,
> VI Washing at their identity.
> Now, helpless in the hollow of
> An unarmorial age, a trough
> Of smoke in slow suspended skeins
> Above their scrap of history,
> Only an attitude remains:
> VII Time has transfigured them into
> Untruth. The stone fidelity
> They hardly meant has come to be
> Their final blazon, and to prove
> Our almost-instinct almost true:
> What will survive of us is love.
>
> *Philip Larkin*

An aside on ... rhyme

We use the alphabet to represent rhyme patterns. Using a letter to represent the sound of the last syllable in each line, you can see that this poem follows a regular rhyme pattern abbcac – the same for each verse.

It is very difficult to write well in this way. Try it!

An aside on ... rhythm

This is the system used to look at poetry that is written in a formal rhyme and rhythm pattern. A line can be divided into 'feet' each containing one accented syllable with one or more unaccented syllables attached to it. If the pattern is two syllables with the stress on the second, this is called an iambic rhythm. This poem uses iambic rhythm.

The earl/ and coun/tess lie/ in stone

This rhythm is the closest to natural speech patterns in English. You will see it in the Shakespeare you are studying, too.

Answer the following questions in as much detail as possible. Use quotations and references to the text to support your ideas.

1 **Verses I and II**

Describe the tomb that the poet is writing about. Why is it different from the usual ones? How does the poet draw our attention to the difference?

_____

_____

_____

_____

2 **Verse III**

Comment on the structure of the first line and the effect created by it. What does the poet suggest about the sculpture in the rest of this verse?

_____

_____

_____

_____

3 **Verse IV**

What is the overall meaning of this verse? Comment on the examples the poet uses.

_____

_____

_____

_____

_____

4 **Verse V**

Identify and comment on the series of images used in this verse.

_____

_____

_____

_____

_____

_____

_____

_____

ISBN 9780170373319

5 **Verse VI**

What is the mood of this verse? How does the poet's choice of words create this mood?

_____

_____

_____

_____

6 **Verse VII**

In your own words, explain the poet's final decision about the tomb as revealed in this verse and its message to us. Do you agree with him?

_____

_____

_____

_____

_____

_____

_____

_____

_____

_____

_____

_____

_____

_____

Text 2

Read the following poem. Look up words you don't know the meaning of and annotate important features (see pages 155-163).

Metaphors

I'm a riddle in nine syllables,
An elephant, a ponderous house,
A melon strolling on two tendrils.
O red fruit, ivory, fine timbers!
This loaf's big with its yeasty rising.
Money's new-minted in this fat purse.
I'm a means, a stage, a cow in calf.
I've eaten a bag of green apples,
Boarded the train there's no getting off.

Sylvia Plath

First ...

On the lines provided below explain in your own words what each metaphor refers to.
Think about:

- how the first line is reflected in the poem's imagery and structure.
- what the final line means.
- how the poet feels about the condition she is in.

1 _____

2 _____

3 _____

4 _____

5 _____

6 _____

7 _____

8 _____

9 _____

ISBN 9780170373319

Answer the following question in as much detail as possible. Use quotations and references to the text to support your ideas.

Explain the way the poem has been structured, its meaning and how the poet is feeling about herself. (Be sure to complete all three parts of this response.)

Read the following poem. Look up words you don't know the meaning of and annotate important features (see pages 155-163).

'In Tenebris' means 'In Darkness'. The poem has a Latin epigraph (brief inscription or quotation usually on a coin, statue etc) from *Psalm 102,* which is written in English in the King James version of the Bible as 'My heart is smitten, and withered like grass'.

In Tenebris

'Percussus sum sicut foenum, et aruit cor meum.'

Wintertime nighs;
But my bereavement-pain
It cannot bring again:
    Twice no one dies.

5   Flower-petals flee;
But, since it once hath been,
No more that severing scene
    Can harrow me.

    Birds faint in dread:
10   I shall not lose old strength
In the lone frost's black length:
    Strength long since fled!

    Leaves freeze to dun;
But friends can not turn cold
15   This season as of old
    For him with none.

    Tempests may scath;
But love can not make smart
Again this year his heart
20   Who no heart hath.

    Black is night's cope;
But death will not appal
One who, past doubtings all,
    Waits in unhope.

Thomas Hardy (1840–1928)

ISBN 9780170373319

Answer the following questions in as much detail as possible. Use quotations and references to the text to support your ideas.

1 How do the poem's title and epigraph prepare you for the content of the poem?

_____

_____

_____

_____

2 Comment on the way the structure of the poem contributes to its meaning.

_____

_____

_____

_____

3 Choose two of these poetic techniques used by the poet: metaphor, coinage, pronouns, imagery. Give example/s and describe the effect of each one you choose.

i _____

_____

_____

ii _____

_____

_____

4 Comment on the word order of the last line of the poem.

_____

_____

_____

5 What is the tone of the poem? Support your answer with reference to the poem.

_____

_____

_____

_____

Read the following poem. Look up words you don't know the meaning of and annotate important features (see pages 155-163).

Death of a Naturalist

All year the flax-dam festered in the heart
Of the townland; green and heavy headed
Flax had rotted there, weighted down by huge sods.
Daily it sweltered in the punishing sun.
Bubbles gargled delicately, bluebottles
Wove a strong gauze of sound around the smell.
There were dragon-flies, spotted butterflies,
But best of all was the warm thick slobber
Of frogspawn that grew like clotted water
In the shade of the banks. Here, every spring
I would fill jampotfuls of the jellied
Specks to range on window-sills at home,
On shelves at school, and wait and watch until
The fattening dots burst into nimble-
Swimming tadpoles. Miss Walls would tell us how
The daddy frog was called a bullfrog
And how he croaked and how the mammy frog
Laid hundreds of little eggs and this was
Frogspawn. You could tell the weather by frogs too
For they were yellow in the sun and brown
In rain.
Then one hot day when fields were rank
With cowdung in the grass the angry frogs
Invaded the flax-dam; I ducked through hedges
To a coarse croaking that I had not heard
Before. The air was thick with a bass chorus.
Right down the dam gross-bellied frogs were cocked
On sods; their loose necks pulsed like sails. Some hopped:
The slap and plop were obscene threats. Some sat
Poised like mud grenades, their blunt heads farting.
I sickened, turned, and ran. The great slime kings
Were gathered there for vengeance and I knew
That if I dipped my hand the spawn would clutch it.

Seamus Heaney

ISBN 9780170373319

First ...

The poem divides naturally into two sections.

Annotate the first section with notes on when and where the event takes place. Look for words that tell you how old the narrator is. Is there any effective imagery, onomatopoeia, similes; any special vocabulary?

Now turn to the second part of the poem. What has happened? What is the dominant image and which words reinforce it? Highlight them. Why does the child think the frogs gathered for vengeance? What does the poem's title add to this part of the narrative? Annotate the poem with your ideas.

When you think you understand the meaning of the poem, answer the following questions in as much detail as possible. Use quotations and references to the text to support your ideas.

1 Is the title comic or serious? Give your reasons.

_____

_____

_____

2 Comment on how the child learns at school and home about frogs.

_____

_____

_____

_____

3 How does the child's imagination make him see the plague of frogs? What does he do?

_____

_____

_____

_____

4 Choose at least one example of onomatopoeia in the poem and explain why the poet has used it.

_____

_____

_____

5 What general comment do you think this poem is making about childhood?

_____

_____

_____

_____

Read the following poem. Look up words you don't know the meaning of and annotate important features (see pages 155-163).

My parents dancing

We, in our fancy dress, were feasting
at long trestles covered in white paper
soon stained by gobs of raspberry jelly
and wet by icecream and icecream spoons.

We had danced in a lightly-controlled fashion
cowboys and fairies, each with their passion
and holding hands passed down along avenues
of garland space and returned to captivity.

Our little energies increased our identities.
Finally, in the Grand Parade, we made a globe
our colours smudged, we ran to eat
at trestle tables, treats piled up.

But on the vacant, vaster floor
more like sea, more like a shore
my parents among the other parents dance
and I cannot forbear to glance

at how they glide and corner and dip
as if, loosing their children, they resume
the leading reins that held between
their forms and passion that adored

and which they leave a space for
as if they too treasure it, leaning away
then irresistibly drawn into its pull
and yet drawing slightly back to accord

it homage. It might be the space
between their twin pillows at night
or a hand's reach behind a head
or her hair that lightly touches his shoulder.

Elizabeth Smither

ISBN 9780170373319

First ...

Read the poem carefully and notice ...

- the subject and style divide between verses 3 and 4
- alliteration
- similes
- metaphor
- words suggesting movement.

When you think you understand the meaning of the poem, answer the following questions in as much detail as possible. Use quotations and references to the text to support your ideas.

1 What is happening in verses 1–3?

_____

_____

_____

2 How does the writer's change of style in verse 4 reflect the ideas in the poem?

_____

_____

_____

_____

_____

3 Comment on the change in focus in lines 13–14

_____

_____

_____

_____

_____

4 What does the child notice about her parents as they dance?

_____

_____

_____

Read the following poem. Look up words you don't know the meaning of and annotate important features (see pages 155-163).

You're Telling Me

Those boring, corny stories
you'll see
they're the ones'll make you weep.

Now when your folks do their reruns,
the Olds' slow same-olds,
their yeah, you've told mes,
you scrape your chair back from the table
that little bit too quickly,
do a cover-up by clearing plates
(you just can't stand that wet look on their faces)
be excused, go to your room,
make your cassette deck dial climb up past that notch
your dad marked off in indelible pen,
rebel in decibels, against—what?
The same-old, whatever they've got.

But you'll cotton on.
Find memory's hereditary,
with its cataleptic seizures
in the middle of the nowhere of your life—
times when you turn to whoever's there to say
did I tell you that one about the night
when my dad just made like a beeline,
jumped dozens of fences for her
to poach hundreds of daffodils
yellow as yolks done in butter,
or how once, in front of everyone,
he sprinted up the down escalator
just to be with her a few minutes sooner?
Or, you'll say, as whoever's gaze it is slips away
the one about how I never did tell him
I'd listened?

Emma Neale

ISBN 9780170373319

First ...

Read the poem carefully and notice ...

- colloquial words
- slang
- clichés
- short lines
- metaphor
- similes
- verse structure.

Answer the following questions in as much detail as possible. Use quotations and references to the text to support your ideas.

1 In verse 2 what is the poet saying about the way teenagers react to their parents' reminiscences?

_____

_____

_____

_____

_____

2 In verse 3 how does she suggest this will change?

_____

_____

_____

_____

3 Summarise the kinds of things she says children will remember. Is she adding her personal memories? How can you tell?

_____

_____

_____

_____

_____

_____

4   Comment on the way the structure of the first and last verses contributes to their meaning.

Think about:
- length of lines
- use of cliché
- change of pronoun.

_____

_____

_____

_____

_____

_____

_____

_____

_____

_____

_____

_____

_____

_____

_____

_____

_____

_____

_____

_____

ISBN 9780170373319

Making connections: texts 5 and 6

It is not unusual to be asked to make comparisons, or to draw connections, between two texts. These two poems do have similarities. We look at the comparison question on page 87. You might like to read this page before you answer this question.

Now that you have analysed texts 5 and 6 answer the following question in as much detail as possible. Use quotations and references to the texts to support your ideas.

Examine the similarities and the differences between Elizabeth Smither's *My Parents Dancing* and Emma Neale's *You're Telling Me*.

An aside on ... using quotations effectively

By this stage of your career as a writer of both longer answers and essays you should be confident in your use of quotations. You should be able to use them to illustrate the points you are making, to support your ideas, rather than just repeating yourself.

Part of the sophistication and depth required at this level is being able to incorporate your quotations into your essay. Here are a few guidelines to help you:

- Put inverted commas at the beginning and the end of the quotation. These show exactly which words are not yours.

- Keep quotations short. If they are short you will be more likely to remember them to use in assessments/exams.

- Be accurate. Use and learn the words exactly as they are used. If you cannot remember them, then paraphrase.

- Quotations should not repeat basic facts already given. Compare these two uses of the same quotation:

   a   In <u>Catcher in the Rye</u> by JD Salinger, the narrator, Holden Caulfield, tells us that he is not going to tell us his life story. 'I'm not going to tell you my whole goddam autobiography or anything.'

   b   In <u>Catcher in the Rye</u> by JD Salinger, the narrator, Holden Caulfield, insists: 'I'm not going to tell you my whole goddam autobiography or anything.'

- Try to embed the quotation into the sentence to embellish the point you are making – this is a more sophisticated technique.

   Holden tells us on the first page that his story will reveal a part of his life that has been disturbing: 'this madman stuff that happened to me last Christmas.'

- Quotations can support your ideas.

   Holden is a teenager; his use of slang 'kind of crap' and exaggeration when referring to his parents 'My parents would have about two haemorrhages apiece ...' reveals his likely age and defensive attitude.

- Quoting from poetry – and this includes much of Shakespeare – requires you to follow certain conventions. Centre the quotation if it is of more than two lines of verse.

   After the fight at the beginning of <u>Romeo and Juliet</u> the Prince criticises the two men who lead the families involved:

   > 'Three civil brawls, bred of an airy word,
   >
   > By thee, old Capulet and Montague,
   >
   > Have thrice disturbed the quiet of our streets'

- Use a / to show the line divide if it is less than two lines long.

   When Romeo first sets eyes on Juliet he is captivated by her; 'Her beauty hangs upon the cheek of night/Like a rich jewel in an Ethiops ear,' he whispers to himself.

One of the things that attracted specific criticism in previous assessment reports from examiners was the 'dumping' of quotations. Use them with finesse!

ISBN 9780170373319

Studying for assessment of your texts

1   Know the text well.

2   Spell its title and author/director's name correctly.

3   Learn a few short quotations that might be used for examples in several essay questions.

4   Know the principal characters' names exactly.

5   List the major theme/themes for revision.

6   Learn details of the setting (time, place, social background).

7   Practise writing to time (you will probably do this in class).

Studying for assessment of unfamiliar texts

The studies on texts that you have completed through the year will have given you the experience of understanding and responding to texts with guidance. In this assessment you have to use those skills without the benefit of a teacher's voice, your fellow classmates' ideas, or a lot of time. It's a great opportunity to show that you CAN read, understand and analyse text all by yourself. Yes, you can.

1   You will have completed several close reading exercises in class (and through *Achievement English @ Year 13*). Revisiting these texts and the questions you were asked and your answers would be useful.

2   Answer the questions again, improving on your first attempt.

3   Make sure you have the process off by heart:

- read the text
- read the questions
- read the text again

- annotate the text (on the page in the assessment, in class if allowed)
- think
- plan
- write.

For some students, this seems like a very long process in an assessment where you just want to get on with answering the question. However, if you follow this process (briskly) you will find that it saves time in the end, because you will know what you want to say when you start to write. It usually means better results, too! Try it out in a class assessment before the real thing.

Using the Internet for study

You will have studied longer texts, like novels and plays, in class. When it comes to writing about these texts it is very tempting to go to the Internet and copy what is written there. It can be very useful to read what others have written, especially if those others are knowledgeable. In fact, if you pick your information wisely you can supplement your class notes and find some new material to refresh your memory about your text. Your teacher may well have recommended useful works of criticism to help you make complete responses about the text you are studying.

However, as you know, there is no quality control on the Internet so what we suggest is:

- Plan your own response to the text first
- Then do some reading of criticism written by others
- Then go back to what you have written and see if you might add to or rework your own ideas.

It's what you think that counts!

7 Language Lists

As a senior student of English you must be able to identify features of language in the text you are studying, whether it be an extract or a complete work. However it is even more important that you are able to explain the effect or contribution these features make to things such as the impact, purpose, structure, theme or tone of the text you are studying.

In this section we are presenting you with a comprehensive list of terminology for you to check what you know, what you recognise but do not fully understand, and what is completely new to you. The techniques are grouped under useful sub-headings:

- Literary
- Grammar and syntax
- Figures of speech
- Parts of speech
- Poetic devices
- Visual
- Film
- Oral

Please note that some terms are not restricted to one grouping. For example, we have listed 'antithesis' and 'tricolon' under Oral because students often meet them when studying speeches. You may also need to use them when close reading a novel, newspaper article or magazine column.

Think about the technical terms that you need to use when you write answers in chemistry – you need similarly precise language to comment successfully on English texts and this list will help you to add depth and detail to your answers.

You will notice that in the left-hand margin there are three circles labelled – 'I know', 'I need to check' and 'I have no idea!' Read through the list and tick the box that best describes your knowledge of each literary term. Use this chapter to increase your personal word bank of literary terminology. By the end of the year we hope every 'I know' box is ticked.

Literary

I know | I need to check | I have no idea

○ ○ ○ **Allegory**
A story or situation written in such a way as to have two coherent meanings. Example: Orwell's *Animal Farm*

○ ○ ○ **Anti-hero**
A protagonist lacking the usual qualities associated with heroes.

○ ○ ○ **Antithesis**
Placing contrasting terms or ideas close together to emphasise their difference and give the effect of balance.
Example: For fools rush in where angels fear to tread.

○ ○ ○ **Apostrophe**
A direct address to a person or personified idea.
Example: *O Romeo, Romeo, wherefore art thou Romeo?*

○ ○ ○ **Archaism**
A word or expression not quite obsolete but no longer in current use.

ISBN 9780170373319

○○○ **Aside**
A dramatic convention in which a participant in the action directly addresses the audience; other characters on the stage are not supposed to hear the aside.

○○○ **Ballad**
A poem or song (which tells a story) in simple, colloquial language.

○○○ **Climax**
The effect of adding one word or phrase to another with increasing importance or impressiveness. It also means 'a series of incidents which rise in dramatic intensity to reach a crisis which is then resolved'.

○○○ **Comedy**
'Comedy' is used most often with reference to a kind of drama which is intended primarily to entertain the audience, and which ends happily for the characters.

○○○ **Dramatic monologue**
A passage in which a single person, not the writer, is speaking.

○○○ **Elegy**
A poem lamenting a person's death eg. Tennyson's *In Memoriam*.

○○○ **Epic**
A long, narrative poem in elevated style about the exploits of superhuman heroes.

○○○ **Genre**
A particular type of text that has distinctive characteristics.
Examples: thriller, romance, science fiction.

○○○ **Irony**
A figure of speech in which the point intended is different from (usually the opposite of) the literal meaning of the words used. Whenever irony is concerned there are two attitudes to the subject: a surface attitude and an underlying attitude.
There are several types of irony:
1. Dramatic irony: occurs when the audience is aware of factors affecting a character that the character is unaware of.
2. Socratic irony: pretending to adopt someone else's viewpoint in order to ridicule them or their ideas.
3. Sarcasm: strong and obvious disapproval given as pretended praise (eg. Hitler was a nice guy)
4. Understatement (or meiosis): here the true magnitude of something is minimised eg. It is sometimes a bit cold at the North Pole.
5. Verbal irony: a figure of speech where the point intended is different from, and usually the opposite (antithesis) of the literal meaning of the words.

○○○ **Light verse**
Poetry that deals with trivial matters or adopts a light-hearted approach to a grave subject.

○○○ **Lyric poetry**
Typically, this is a short poem where the poet expresses personal feelings, usually about love.

○○○ **Metonymy**
The substitution of one word for another closely associated with it. eg. The crown will find an heir.

○○○ **Narrative verse**
Poetry that tells a story.

○○○ **Ode**
A long lyric poem with intricate stanza forms, seriousness of purpose and grandeur of style.

○○○ **Oxymoron**
Two words or phrases or opposite or contrasting meaning placed together for effect.
Example: Parting is such sweet sorrow.

○○○ **Parody**
An imitation of a specific work of literature devised so as to ridicule its characteristic features.

○○○ **Protagonist**
The person the story is about.

○○○ **Revenge tragedy**
A special form of tragedy which concentrates on the protagonist's pursuit of vengeance against those who have done him wrong eg. *Hamlet*.

○○○ **Satire**
Literature which exhibits or examines vice and folly and makes them appear ridiculous or contemptible.

○○○ **Soliloquy**
A monologue spoken by the characters on the stage; usually it either indicates what is to happen later in the play or expresses the innermost thoughts of the speaker.

○○○ **Sonnet**
A lyric poem of fixed form: 14 lines of iambic pentameter, rhymed and organised according to several intricate schemes. In general the ideas developed in a sonnet accord loosely with these divisions, which are marked by rhyme.

○○○ **Tragedy**
A play that traces the career and downfall of an individual, and shows in their downfall both the capacities and limitations of human life.

Grammar and syntax

○○○ **Apostrophe (')**
Has two main purposes: the first to show ownership; the second to show omitted letters within a contraction.
Example: My friend's father offered to pay for me, which wasn't a good idea at all.

○○○ **Brackets ( )**
Most commonly used to include extra information within a sentence.
Example: She said to me (for the millionth time), 'Go on, have a go.'

I know
I need to check
I have no idea

I know
I need to check
I have no idea

Clause
A group of words containing a finite verb (ie. a verb with a subject) in a sentence of two or more finite verbs. If there is only one finite verb in a sentence we call it a simple sentence. A main clause is an independent one, but a sub-ordinate clause is dependent (on a main clause).

Colon (:)
Introduces more information or shows divisions.
Example: I have lots of reasons: I'm too scared, I'm too poor, I'm not interested, the rope might break, I value my life!

Comma (,)
Tells the reader when to take a short pause in a sentence.
Example: I was supposed to do a bungy jump, but then I decided I was too scared.

Complex sentence
One main clause joined to one or more subordinate clauses. A writer uses a complex sentence to express an idea that requires more elaboration.
Example: The student asked a question when he had a problem with his classwork.

Compound sentence
Two or more main clauses (simple sentences) joined together with a conjunction or separated by a semi-colon. A compound sentence gives us more information than a simple sentence by developing a basic idea.
Example: The student asked a question and the teacher answered it.

Compound-complex sentence
Two or more main clauses linked to one or more subordinate clauses.
Example: The student asked a question and the teacher answered it because the teacher knew the student needed help.

Contraction
A word shortened in speech or spelling eg. He would've.

Dash (–)
Has three main purposes: the first to indicate a sudden change of thought; the second to lead to the unexpected; the third to give extra information.
Example: I couldn't get out of it – but wait – maybe there was another way.

Demonstratives
Words such as 'this', 'that', 'these' followed by a noun, as in 'this book'.

Exclamation mark (!)
Used at the end of a sentence that shows strong feeling.
Example: 'I would never do something so stupid!'

Hyphens (-)
Used to join two or more words to make a compound word and to divide words at the end of a line.
Example: I looked straight into the eyes of my so-called best friend.

Inverted commas ("")
Inverted commas (speech marks) are used to show the words being said by a speaker. Only the actual words spoken go inside the speech marks.
Example: 'OK, I'll do it, but only if you come with me – in tandem!' 'You're on!' she whooped. 'Let's go!'

Minor sentence
A sentence without a completed verb that is often used for emphasis. Many common greetings are also minor sentences. Minor sentences are frequently used in advertising as they give a passage an informal, casual, clipped, fast tone. They also emphasise key words within the sentence.
Example: (1) Hello. (2) Never in a million years.

Paradox
This is a statement whose parts seem mutually contradictory, yet which make sense after deeper consideration.
Example: Deep down he's really shallow.

Question mark (?)
Used at the end of a sentence (or clause) that asks a direct question.

Semi-colon (;)
Used to break up long sentences and lists or join clauses that are closely related.
Example: My close friend told me I should try it; but she wasn't going to do it herself.

Simple sentence
A group of words, including a verb, that makes sense on its own. Simple sentences are commonly used to describe a single idea.
Example: The student asked a question.

Figures of speech

Allusion
A reference to something related indirectly to the subject matter of prose or poetry. Example: 'I am tied to the stake, and I must stand the course.' An allusion to bear-baiting (King Lear).

Coinage
The making of new words for a special purpose: much favoured in advertising. Example: Donut (doughnut), Schweppervescence etc.

Extended metaphor
The comparison between two things is continued beyond the first point of comparison. This technique extends and deepens a description.
Example:
How long have they tugged the leash, and strained apart,
My pack of unruly hounds! I cannot start
Them again on a quarry of knowledge they hate to hunt,
(from Last Lesson of the Afternoon, D.H. Lawrence)

Hyperbole
A deliberate exaggeration used to emphasise a feeling or produce a humorous effect. Example: I could eat a horse.

ISBN 9780170373319

I know
I need to check
I have no idea

I know
I need to check
I have no idea

I know
I need to check
I have no idea

○○○ **Imperative**
A phrase used to express a request, order or command.
Example: Go to bed now.

○○○ **Metaphor**
A form of comparison (see Simile). Instead of using 'like' or 'as', a metaphor says the two things are the same.
Example: My brother John is a pig. (This suggests that John has unpleasant manners, not that he literally is a pig.)

○○○ **Pun**
An expression that plays on different meanings of the same word or phrase. It may draw attention to an idea or create a humorous effect.
Example: Mercutio, mortally wounded, says: 'Ask for me tomorrow and you shall find me a grave man.'

○○○ **Rhetorical question**
A question that is designed to make a vivid suggestion rather than demand an answer. The writer or speaker is inviting the agreement of the audience.

○○○ **Simile**
A phrase that compares two things, using 'like' or 'as'. A simile works by suggesting the two things have characteristics that are similar. Similes add colour and vitality to writing.
Example: My brother John eats like a pig. (This suggests that John has unpleasant table manners.)

Other

○○○ **Accent**
Intonation and pronunciation of words characteristic of a group.

○○○ **Colloquial**
An adjective used to describe everyday, spoken language which is generally informal. It is usually regarded as inappropriate in formal writing.
Example: 'Let's have a go at Hymn 96' would be inappropriate for use in a church service as it is colloquial.

○○○ **Connotation**
The implied or suggested meaning of a word.

○○○ **Denotation**
The dictionary meaning of a word.

○○○ **Dialect**
The given name to a language as it is spoken in a particular region of a country, having its local peculiarities of vocabulary, pronunciation, and turn of phrase.

○○○ **Dialogue**
Conversation as opposed to monologue (one speaker), narrative, descriptive writing, etc. 'Duologue' means 'restricted to two persons' and 'polylogue' means multi-participant conversation.

○○○ **Jargon**
Specialised language used by people who work together or share a common interest. The advantage of using jargon is that it helps people communicate quickly and effectively with each other as they do not have to use long-winded explanations and definitions.
Examples: hard drive, RAM, hyperlink (computer language).

○○○ **Slang**
Words or expressions that belong to a particular group of people. In most cases slang is unacceptable as appropriate language. You should only use slang in your English work if it is appropriate to both the character and the situation.
Example: It was awesome, ace, massive! (teenage slang).

Parts of speech

○○○ **Adjective**
A describing word. It adds meaning to a noun by giving more information. A comparative adjective provides a comparison between two things and a superlative adjective between three or more.
Example: *big* dog … *bigger* dog … *biggest* dog.

○○○ **Adverb**
A word that tells us how, when or where an action takes place. Its job is to give extra meaning to verbs.
Example: Tomorrow I will build a snowman outside, *carefully*.

○○○ **Antonym**
A word that is opposite in meaning to another word.
Example: deep – shallow.

○○○ **Conjunction**
A word that joins words or sentences. Conjunctions help give variety to your writing by allowing you to have sentences of different length.
Example: The girl met the boy *and* they went for a walk on the beach.

○○○ **Noun**
A naming word. It refers to a thing, person, animal, substance, quality or place.

○○○ **Prefix**
One or more letters added to the beginning of a word to alter its meaning or form a new word.
Example: appear – *dis*appear.

○○○ **Preposition**
A word that tells us the position or place of something in relation to something else.
Example: The cat sat *on* the mat.

○○○ **Pronoun**
A word that may be used instead of a noun. Writers use pronouns to save repeating a person's name too often in a sentence or passage. Some pronouns are used to make the reader feel involved in the passage, as though the writer is talking directly to him or her.
Example: *You* know how *it* feels to quarrel with *your* best friend.

○○○ **Suffix**
One or more letters added to the end of a word to alter its meaning.
Example: grace – grace*ful*, nation – nation*al*.

I know	I need to check	I have no idea

○○○ **Synonym**
A word identical or very similar in meaning to another word. It is important to look at synonyms as they help to improve your writing and vocabulary by adding variety.
Example: hot – spicy

○○○ **Verb**
A doing or being word.
Example: (1) I *walked* to school today. (2) I *was* happy.

Poetic devices

○○○ **Alliteration**
The repetition of consonant sounds, usually at the start of the word. Writers use alliteration for several reasons: it helps draw our attention to a line in a poem or passage, or a particular image, and it can slow down our reading or speed up the words in order to create an atmosphere. The last reason, usually employed by advertisers, is that it can make things easy to remember.
Example: 'A black-backed gull bent like an iron bar' has to be read slowly in order to pronounce the bs. Therefore it emphasises the strength of the wind against which the bird is flying.

○○○ **Anacoluthon**
A change in grammatical structure, as in the following example: 'Is he still waiting ... of course, you told me yesterday.'

○○○ **Assonance**
The deliberate repetition of the same vowel sound followed by a different consonant sound. Assonance may create a musical effect, or be used to highlight imagery.
Example: 'He climbed high, singing wildly,
Clinging to the rock face
Alive, at last.'

○○○ **Blank verse**
Verse with a set rhythm but no set rhyme scheme.

○○○ **Caesura**
A natural pause or a break within a line of poetry, usually indicated by a punctuation mark.

○○○ **Cliché**
An expression that has lost its originality and humour through constant use. The English language is full of clichés, often expressed as metaphors or similes.

○○○ **Emotive language**
Language that attempts to play on people's emotions.
Example: The shopping centre was littered with decaying food scraps, empty torn plastic packets, broken glass, dumped supermarket trolleys and sad, defeated people. (The language chosen here is to make the shopping centre seem depressing.)

○○○ **End-stopped line**
The lines of a stanza that have a grammatical pause at the end of each line. This technique completes an idea visually and grammatically.

○○○ **Enjambment**
When the meaning of a line of poetry is completed on the next line. This technique can emphasise an idea or add to the rhythm of and flow of the lines.

○○○ **Eye rhymes**
Words which are spelled alike and in most instances were once pronounced alike, but now have a different pronunciation: prove-love, daughter-laughter.

○○○ **Iambic pentameter**
The metre used by Shakespeare in blank verse or in sonnets. It consists of 5 iambic feet.

○○○ **Imagery**
The creation of images or pictures to help writers achieve their intended purpose.

○○○ **Metre**
Is the generally regular repetition of a given pattern of accented and unaccented syllables; the metrical unit is the foot. See also rhythm.

○○○ **Onomatopoeia**
When the sound of the word imitates or suggests the meaning or noise of the action described.
Example: The *buzz* of the chainsaw.

○○○ **Personification**
When a non-living thing is given living characteristics or when a non-human thing is given human characteristics.
Example: The vine is strangling that tree. (This gives the idea of vine as aggressor with intent to harm and the tree as the victim.)

○○○ **Repetition**
Where words and/or phrases are repeated for emphasis or special effect.
Example: It was cold that night, very, very cold.

○○○ **Rhyme**
The repetition of similar sounds. It is often used in order to be pleasing to the ear and to give a piece of writing rhythm and flow. Rhyme is also used to hold certain lines of poetry together in order to link ideas and images.
Example: She left the web, she left the loom, (from *The Lady of Shallot*, Alfred Lord Tennyson).

○○○ **Rhythm**
The pace or tempo at which a passage moves. Rhythm reflects the underlying emotion or meaning of a passage. It is created by the emphasis or stress placed on syllables, or words, or groups of words. It can be referred to as 'metre'. In the example below the beat/sound of the train is imitated.
Example: This is the night mail crossing the border
Bringing the cheque and the postal order (from *The Night Mail*, W.H. Auden).

○○○ **Point of view**
The angle from which a piece is written. A passage may be written from its author's point of view or a narrator's point of view or an institution's point of view.

○○○ **Purpose**
The reason why a passage has been written.
Examples: to inform, to amuse, to persuade or to promote a particular action.

ISBN 9780170373319

Setting
Time, place, social background.

Sibilance
The repetition of the consonant 's' and 'z' to give a hissing sound. The effect of sibilance is to slow the reader as 's' and 'z' take longer to say. This, in turn, emphasises the idea and can also create an onomatopoeic effect. Example: suggesting snake-like movement and sound – 'slippery, slithering, sliding snake'.

Style
The way a piece has been written.

Symbolism
A word or phrase signifying a sign or mark representing something else. A symbol brings a significant idea and all its connotations through use of a single word. Example: The dove (of peace), the cross (of Christianity)

Target audience
The section of the viewing public that a piece is largely aimed at or pitched to. It may be an age group, gender or ethnic group.
Example: Hairy Maclary books are targeted at preschool children.

Theme
The main ideas that the author/director wants us to think about.

Tone
The writer's attitude about the topic of the piece. It may be angry, sarcastic, passionate or sad, and so on.

Visual

Audience
The designer of an image always takes into account the intended audience in order to use techniques that are likely to attract that particular group. They may be female or male, teenagers or older, ethnic groups or movie-goers.

Balance
Images aim to present a balanced effect – achieved by thinking of the space in thirds, quarters, or halves, each section needing similar proportions or elements.

Bold lines
Some features may be outlined to give them definition. Framing the image may also help keep the viewer's eye focused.

Border
Used to create an edge to an image. It focuses the viewer's eye on the page. A border can reflect the image's content, for example koru shapes on a poster for a Māori film.

Colour
Designers carefully select which colours they use on a static image. Designers also need to consider whether there are colours that will help represent their idea. For example, yellow usually represents warmth or happiness whereas black can represent sophistication or death.

Contrast
One method of gaining people's attention is by using two colours for eye-catching contrasts. Contrast can also be achieved by juxtaposing a picture with an area of text.

Dominant visual feature
The feature that first grabs a viewer's attention. Designers think carefully about what it is they first want people to see as it often affects whether they will look at the image more closely. It may be a picture, words or part of an illustration.

Emotive language
Words that are aimed at stirring emotion. Anger? Distress? Joy?

Empty space
There are times when empty space becomes an important technique. Empty space around the words and pictures helps to draw attention to them.

Euphemism
Saying something unpleasant in a pleasant way. Euphemisms often use positive connotations instead of negative. i.e. slender instead of scrawny, cuddly instead of fat.
Example: 'A deodorant for moist underarm areas.'

Hyperbole
Exaggeration for effect, usually to grab your attention.
Example: Russell Hobbs – 'generations ahead'.

Impact
An image needs to stand out amongst a crowd of other images. The image may be shocking, dramatic, unusual, funny or controversial.

Imperative/command
The use of a command to provoke actions. Advertisements are written to persuade us to act so it is not surprising the imperative is used frequently. We are asked to 'try', 'use', 'look', 'hurry on down', etc. These add force to the suggestions being made and are also designed to make it seem urgent that we buy the product.

Layout
How the words and pictures of an image have been put together. Everything is placed in order to create a unity of ideas and let the viewer's eye move naturally from the most important feature to the least.

Lettering
There are many options available with lettering: different fonts, sizes, upper or lower case, italic or bold. If an image needs to be seen from a distance then it needs to have large lettering; if the image is going to be held in a hand, such as an advertisement or flyer, there is more choice.

Message
The ideas contained in the image. The basic aim of an image may be to influence us to act a certain way or make a particular decision. It may be to sponsor a World Vision child, buy one product over another or attend a particular tertiary institute.

○○○ Neologisms
The language of advertising has contributed a generous share of new words into the English language. While purists might frown, these words sometimes achieve quite extensive use. We are invited to 'unzip' a banana or sip a drink that is 'orangemostest', or taste the 'Schweppervesence'. Neologisms help make a product appear original and retain the consumers' attention as they read the advertisement. They may also be referred to as coinage.
Many of the emotive adjectives first found their way into the world through advertising. For example: bubbly, minty, tangy, chewy, nutty, silky and spicy.

○○○ Perspective
Images can be two dimensional (look flat) or three dimensional (have depth). You can suggest perspective on a 2D image or build depth by embossing or shadowing.

○○○ Pictures/illustrations
It is important that a picture or visual be clear and that it is a suitable size. The chosen picture also needs to be appropriate to the image – it would be silly to use a picture of a baby to advertise a retirement village!

○○○ Proportion
The graphic elements in an image should be in correct ratio to each other. For example, a person's head should match the size of his or her body. Proportion may be distorted for comic or dramatic effect.

○○○ Reverse print
White text on a black background (reversing the usual black text on white). Reverse print is used to make the lettering stand out.

○○○ Slogan
A catchphrase often linked to a company or product. For example, Nike – 'Just do it!' or The Warehouse – 'Where everyone gets a bargain'.

○○○ Symbol
This is a word or set of words that signifies an object or event which itself signifies something else.
Example: The cross symbolises the Christian religion
The colour white represents purity and innocence.

○○○ Tone
The mood of the writing. Personal? Colloquial? Formal? Slang?

○○○ Unusual images
An unusual picture or layout may make people stop and look more carefully at an image. Designers are always trying to come up with new and interesting ways to catch the audience's attention.

○○○ Use of statistics
Factual information often helps to sway a person's opinion.

○○○ Well-known/popular faces
People like to buy something that others endorse, particularly if they know something about the product or topic. For example, Hamish Carter would be a good person to use to sell running shoes as he has a reputation as a runner.

Film

○○○ Close-up (CU)
Contains no background but focuses on the whole of an object or a person's head and shoulders. They may reveal human emotions or private information.

○○○ Cut
A change from one shot to the next without using an effect such as a dissolve, wipe or fade.

○○○ Dissolve
Occurs when one frame is gradually replaced by another so that at the mid-point of the dissolve both are visible on the screen. They can be used to show a change of location or time, but they are also used to indicate a flashback or a dream, or to show what a character is thinking.

○○○ Editing
The post-production process where the film stock is assembled to achieve the final product. Shots and scenes are selected, arranged and ordered in the most dramatic way.

○○○ Establishing shot (extreme long shot – ELS)
Contains a lot of landscape and gives important information about the setting, atmosphere or context in which following events will take place. It is often used at the beginning of a scene or sequence.

○○○ Extreme close-up (ECU)
Focuses on an aspect of an object in great detail or a part of a person's face, headline of a newspaper or detail of symbols such as a police identification.

○○○ Fade
Where the screen is black at the beginning, then gradually the image appears. A fade-out is the opposite of this. A fade can be used to suggest a passage of time, or a new location. It also suggests a special relationship between the two scenes that would not be conveyed by a simple cut.

○○○ Full shot (FS)
Contains the whole height of any figure in the frame.

○○○ High-angle shot
Taken when the camera is above or looking down at the figure. The main purpose of this shot is to make the object or person look small, insignificant or helpless.

ISBN 9780170373319

I know
I need to check
I have no idea

Long shot (LS)
Contains a fair amount of landscape or background though figures in the scene are recognisable as being human and male or female.

Low-angle shot
Taken when the camera is below or looking up at a figure. The main purpose of this shot is to make the object or person look large, powerful and dominant.

Medium shot (mid shot – MS)
Where the person is seen from the waist up. If there are two people in the shot it is called a two-shot, if there are three, a three-shot.

Over-the-shoulder shot
Where a shot is filmed over a character's shoulder from behind. It is usual for this shot to look towards another character and will generally be followed by a reverse-angle shot showing the face of the person whose back was to the camera. It is mostly used during conversations or interviews.

Overhead shot
Taken when the camera is directly above the figure.

Pan
When a camera moves horizontally (side to side) on its tripod. It is often used to show the vastness of a location.

Point-of-view (POV) shot
Where the camera becomes the eyes of one of the characters and sees things from that character's point of view.

Tilt
Where the camera moves upwards or downwards on its tripod to follow moving objects or reveal a scene or object which is too big to fit in one frame.

Tracking
The camera (mounted on tracks, vehicle, dolly or hand-held) follows the subject. You will frequently see this shot used during a 'chase' scene as it makes the camera appear to be following or 'tracking' the object: it makes the audience feel like they are alongside the action.

Under shot
Taken when the camera is directly underneath the figure. This suggests extreme power or danger.

Wipe
Occurs when one shot is covered up or replaced by another shot moving horizontally across the screen. A wipe is used as a transition from one scene to another and suggests a close relationship between the images.

Oral

Allusion/reference
Covert, implied, indirect reference (to something or someone). For example: 'fourscore and seven years ago' alludes to the Bible in its language; 'founding forefathers' alludes to USA history

Anecdotes
Short stories used to help illustrate a point.

Antithesis
The contrast between words or ideas. Used to emphasise a difference and/or to give the effect of balance.
For example: 'He knew everything about literature except how to enjoy it.' (*Catch 22* by Joseph Heller)

Audience appeal
A good speaker knows his/her audience before he/she begins and reads his/her audience as he/she speaks. A student wanting to be voted onto his/her school's Board of Trustees will talk about current issues facing students at that school. An aspiring politican wanting to be voted in by a community facing a major issue (eg., West Coast: logging, Waihi: mining) will talk about that issue above all else.

Body language
How a speaker stands and moves. The use of body language adds interest to a speech.

Emotive words
Add impact to a speech.

Examples/statistics
These are best used to support an argument. If they are 'shocking' they can help capture an audience's attention and keep them listening.

Eye-contact
Establishes a rapport and makes an audience feel involved.

Gesture
They can add interest and help emphasise a point. Think of speech-making as having an animated conversation with a friend.

Humour
A great ice-breaker and an effective tool for keeping an audience listening if linked to either the topic, audience or the occasion.

Intonation
This is the way the voice rises and falls while speaking and adds atmosphere and mood.

Listing
Including many examples in a list form may add weight to your argument.

ISBN 9780170373319

I know
I need to check
I have no idea

○ ○ ○ **Parallelism**
Comparison or correspond-ence of two successive passages:
'On the 4th of July we count our blessings, and there are so many to count. We're thankful for the families we love. We're thankful for the opportunities in America. We're thankful for our free-dom ...'
(George W. Bush, 4 July 2002.)

○ ○ ○ **Pause**
Useful for emphasising important points. It can also create suspense or be used for dramatic effect as well as offering an easy place to maintain eye-contact.

I know
I need to check
I have no idea

○ ○ ○ **Personal pronouns**
These make a speech more personal and help the audi-ence feel involved.

○ ○ ○ **Quotations**
Sayings that sum up in a nutshell what a speaker wishes to convey are useful devices. Proverbs are particularly useful in this way.
For example: 'The hand that rocks the cradle rules the world.' 'Where there's a will there's a way.'
A well-known phrase is also often a cliché – repeated too often to have much effect. A quotation can give a speech an air of greater authority.

I know
I need to check
I have no idea

○ ○ ○ **Tricolon**
The division of an idea into three harmonious parts, usually of increasing power. For example:
'... government of the people, by the people, for the people' (Abraham Lincoln, President of the USA, in the Gettysburg Address at the dedication of a graveyard at Gettysburg, one of the battlefields of the American Civil War in 1863.)
'Today, our fellow citizens, our way of life, our very free-dom came under attack ...'
(George Bush, President of the USA, in his address to the nation after the terrorist attack on New York, 11 September 2001.)

Use this space to list any additional language techniques introduced to you by your teacher.

ISBN 9780170373319